THE
LIFE
I DIDN'T
EXPECT

Facing Adversity and Winning

By Ray Cerda, Jr.

Printed in the United States of America

ISBN: 978-1-07-652112-5

First Trade paperback edition in 2019.

Author Consultant and Editing: Michael Gray
Cover Design: Carl at ExtendedImagery.com
Text Design and Composition: Rick Soldin

Author photo used with permission from Ray Cerda, Jr. and the City of Irving

All photos from the Ray Cerda, Jr. Family Collection and the Joyce Read Family Collection with permission.

Paperback Printed by Amazon – Kindle Direct Publishing
eBook distributed by Amazon – Kindle Direct Publishing

This is a true story. The names of some characters, locations, and situations have been changed.

To Mom and Dad: You've given me so much love and guidance. I hope I've made you proud of the person I've become.

To my immediate family: Ninfa, Chonny, Elizabeth, Michael, Nikki, Debbie, Jimmy, Dalton, Morgan, Connor, Lynne, and David: You gave your all to me when I had nothing to give in return. Family is everything.

To my relatives and close friends: You always have my back.

~Ray

Contents

Chapter One

May 22, 1981

It was fourth down on the thirty-five-yard line for quarterback Ray Cerda. His team was up by six and barely hanging on. Ray rubbed his hands, making sure they were dry, and glanced at the clock for the third time.

One minute forty-three seconds left, he thought. *Man, that's a lifetime for most teams.*

He'd seen some high school teams score with six seconds left. A tiny slip by the cornerback or an arm tackle busted and *boom!* Kick the extra point and the game would be over.

"They're out of timeouts," the referee said to the head coach.

Ray chewed on his bottom lip. All he needed was seven yards for a first down and it was victory formation time. But it was going to be a *long* seven yards.

His head coach stood next to him, studying a chart. It was too risky to attempt a field goal, especially since they had missed two extra points. And there had been too many blocked kicks in practice to think some high school kid could get the ball up and bang through a fifty-two-yarder. No, this was an easy decision.

"Okay, Ray," the head coach said, "I'm putting the game in your hands. Slot R 36K on two. Do it!"

Ray nodded and ran back to the huddle, dropping to a knee. "Listen up. This is the game. Do your job and give me a chance to do mine. We're going to win this game right here."

His teammates nodded.

"Slot R 36K on two. Break!"

Ray wiped his hands on the dirty towel hanging from his waist-band as the players took their positions. *Slot R 36K*, he thought. *A run-pass option. Fake a handoff to the running back to suck in the defensive end. Then pull the ball out and throw it to the tight end, eight yards down on the right side. If he's covered, look beyond him to the receiver. Hopefully, he'll be open. Worst-case scenario, use that all-district track speed and run for it.*

The referee blew the whistle, starting the play clock. Ray drew in a deep breath and exhaled slowly. The smell of fresh-cut grass. The sweat stinging his forehead. The glare from the stadium lights. It was for this very moment that he'd spent so much time training, turning his body into a finely tuned athletic machine. At sixteen, with lightning bolts for legs and a deep football knowledge embedded in his brain by his father, he needed welder's goggles to see through his bright future. Everyone knew he had a lifetime of achievements ahead of him. Actually, they expected it.

Now, he just had to make one play.

Ray approached the line and looked over the defense. The end, the one he had to watch, dug in harder. *With the count on two, he might jump. Fourth and two is much easier than fourth and seven.*

Ray put his hands under the center and stiffened. "Hut!" he yelled, but no one jumped.

He peeked at the cornerback to the right, then glanced to the left. He held his gaze there, hoping to draw the defense to that side.

"Hut!" he cried, and the ball was in his hands.

Ray dropped back and pivoted to his left, shoving the ball in the tailback's midsection. As the back's arms clamped down on it, the defensive end bulled his way between the right guard and tackle, aiming for the back. Ray jerked the ball out and spun to his right.

8

A loud crunch exploded from behind as the end tackled the back, landing on top of him with an elbow to the neck. Ray ignored it. He was too focused on locating his tight end.

There he is. But he's covered.

Suddenly, a linebacker dressed in solid black appeared. Ray sensed him chewing up yards, closing the distance between them. Having already taken several hits from this sledgehammer, Ray was determined to avoid the punishment. He had to buy more time. Unfortunately, this maniac had the angle. Ray ran to the right, but was almost out of space and time.

In a split second, he picked up the gold uniform of his receiver. He was giving Ray a small gap—maybe a foot—between his man and the cornerback. This was his best chance. Ray came to a full stop, planted his feet, and let the ball go. Still in his follow-through, the linebacker smashed into Ray's chest, sending him to the ground.

Just like that, none of it mattered anymore. Ray's mouth opened, trying to suck air back into his lungs like a fish trapped on land. The cheers of the crowd in the distance faded from his mind, replaced by a strange static. Lying flat on his back, all he could see were the stadium lights. They glowed against the dark May sky. He thought about the intersection of B and E hallway. He had stopped there earlier that morning and accepted good luck wishes from several students. He would've signed autographs if they'd asked him, but he'd had to get to math class. He had bounded up the steps like a jackrabbit, hurrying so he wouldn't be late to Mrs. Wyndham's class. After all, there was only one more week of class left.

Summer's almost here, he thought, blinking to clear the spots from his vision.

The crowd roared. All Ray could do was listen as time stood still.

He felt a rough hand shake his shoulder and looked up to find a lineman reaching down to help him. The static in his mind grew louder as he tried to move his arm.

The lineman frowned, bending over to look him square in the face. "Hey, you all right?"

Ray blinked a few more times, suddenly feeling a trickle of air slide down his throat into his lungs. Then it turned into a waterfall. As he sputtered and fought to catch his breath, the static faded and his fingers and toes finally became unstuck. He sat up, realizing he was in a circle of celebrating teammates.

"Man, what a pass!" the center said, beaming as he helped Ray to his feet. "That was perfect. The only spot that would've worked."

Ray noticed the scoreboard. Gold 18 | Black 6. They were going to win. Victory was sweet!

●——●

Coach Stalcup picked up a sheet of paper, looking through columns of colored statistics. He was reviewing this when his quarterback walked into the office.

"Coach, you wanted to talk to me?"

"Yeah, Ray, close the door." Coach Stalcup waited until the door clicked. An assistant coach stood next to him, giving Ray a grin. "Each spring, the Black and Gold game gives us a chance to look at all our players—especially our quarterbacks. With your performance tonight, *you* are our quarterback."

Ray beamed. "Thanks, Coach. I promise I'll do my best for you and this team."

"I know you will. You've put in three years of hard work and it's your time. I expect big things from you this fall. Before we get to that, though, we have to fix a few things. We'll start back in August and get you ready. Then we'll let you lead us to the playoffs as our starting senior quarterback. I want you to have fun this summer, but work hard. You only get so many summers before life reaches up and smacks you in the face."

"I know, Coach. Me and my girlfriend have a lot of plans. But I'll be in top shape when we start training camp. Trust me, I'm excited and I'll be ready."

"Good. Hit the showers." As Ray turned to leave, Coach Stalcup stopped him. "Hey, I hear you boys are headed to the lake for some team bonding. Right?"

Ray's smile dimmed. "Yes, but my parents won't let me. I'm going to try and talk them into it."

Coach Stalcup pointed the sheet of statistics at him. "If you go, be careful. I don't need you getting injured. Understand?"

Ray nodded. "Absolutely. I'm always careful, especially with the parents I have. They practically keep me in a bubble. And just to make sure, they warn me pretty much every day not to do anything stupid or dangerous."

"Okay. That makes me feel better. Now, go and have a great summer!"

The door closed and Coach Stalcup turned to the assistant. "That kid is something else. Class president, honor roll, and those track records he just set. With his speed, we're going to surprise a lot of folks. They won't even see us coming."

"You're right. His dad has been diagramming plays for him since he was a kid. Add in the family gene pool like Chonny. Remember him? That boy was half man half monster! Even his sister Debbie tore it up on the softball field."

"I guess we'll have a front row seat to it all. Maybe, just maybe, the Cerda family can take us to state."

•——•

Ray cruised through the streets of Irving, the sound cranked up in his orange Chevy pickup. With his air conditioning spotty, he kept the windows down. This let the warm May breeze swirl around in the

11

cab, cooling him while carrying Boston's "More Than a Feeling" out the window.

He tried to focus on which pitch he'd make to his parents, but thoughts of his girlfriend kept getting in the way. Anyone who knew Allison Taylor would understand. She was super cute, popular, a great student, and a terrific athlete. Allison was his first true love. He knew they were still young, but maybe they'd keep it together and get married. He could always hope.

Ray pulled his '73 pickup into the driveway, making sure he could easily back out if his parents bought his pitch. Grabbing his bag, he bounded up the steps and burst through the front door, spotting his mother coming out of the kitchen.

"Great game, Ray," she said. "We're so proud of you."

It was pitch time. "Thanks, Mom. All the guys asked if I was going to the lake. I told them my parents wouldn't let me. They didn't believe me so they're coming over to hear it firsthand."

"We talked about this. Nothing good happens at the lake. Chonny never went to the lake."

Ray's father stepped out of the bedroom. "Yeah, we've covered this, son."

"I know, Dad, but please. I'm begging you! I had a great game. The guys want to bond—you know, be a team." He left off the part about his girlfriend. She didn't want him to go either.

Ray, Sr. shook his head. "I don't think so."

His sister Debbie came out to congratulate him. She was home for the summer, her classes at San Angelo State over for the semester. "Hey, I brought you a cake to celebrate your victory."

The doorbell rang, diverting Ray's attention. He opened the door so his friends could pile into the living room. With the noise level increasing, Ray's mother came in with a frown.

"Mrs. Cerda," a player said, "is it true Ray can't come to the lake?"

Maria bit her lip. "I don't know."

Ray, Jr. spotted the doubt creeping over her face. *I'm almost there.*

"Come on," the player said. "Everyone's going. Ray's our quarterback. You can't have team bonding without Ray."

She turned to her husband. "What do you think?"

He shook his head again. Before he could speak, his son and two players surrounded him, their pleas unrelenting.

"Fine," Ray Sr. said. "I guess you can go. But listen up. Go to the lake and don't leave there, no matter what. Do you understand?"

"Sure, Dad."

"And please, son," his mother said, "don't drink and drive. Please!"

"I won't, Mom. I promise."

Before she could say another word, he sprinted to his room and grabbed a bag he'd packed the day before—just in case. "Come on, guys. Let's go!" Ray wanted to take yes for an answer before it turned into a no. It had happened before.

Ray darted outside and was met by Craig Belden coming up the steps. "Did your parents say yes?" Craig asked.

"They did. You driving?"

"You bet," Craig replied.

Behind him, Ray saw the other players making their way back to their cars. His mother stood on the front step, still chewing on her lip. Her hand rose in a weak wave, and Ray waved back as Craig's pickup pulled away. A mile down the road, Craig lowered the radio. "Man, your parents sure are protective. Your mom looked like she'd never see you again."

"That's the story of my life," Ray said dramatically. "They worry about *everything.*"

"Thank God I don't have to live like that."

As they neared Lake Grapevine, Craig slowed to a crawl. "See if you can spot the dirt road that leads to the lake."

"There it is," Ray said, pointing.

"Got it." Craig made a safe left turn off the two-lane Highway 114 and accelerated. With no rain in several weeks, the gravel was loose. Out of nowhere, the rough road bent sharply to the left.

"Whoa!" Ray said as the truck fishtailed toward a massive oak tree. Gripping the door handle, he prepared for the impact on his side.

Craig spun the wheel in the direction of the tree, straightening out the truck and regaining control. "Sorry about that," Craig said. "Who would put a bend like that in a dirt road?"

"Someone who didn't want to cut down that old tree," Ray said, shaking his head. *Man, that was close.*

The two football players arrived safely at the remote campground to find a large fire with dozens of players relaxing around it. Ray high-fived several buddies before spreading out his sleeping bag and sitting down. It didn't take long before beer cans made the rounds along with sodas and water. Wisps of different smoke floated up from more than a few mouths. As the locusts and crickets buzzed, the night ticked on.

Ray leaned over to Craig. "Hey, it's kind of boring here. Susan Hatfield is having that swim party over at her house. Want to go?"

It had been two hours of sitting around a fire and talking to his teammates. Four or five girls had appeared, peeling off with their boyfriends and disappearing in the darkness. For the ones left, there wasn't much to do but stare at the embers rising up from the crackling fire.

"That's a drill team party," Craig said. "We aren't invited, right?"

"Come on, they told me about it for a reason. They'll let me in. But you? I may have to beg."

"Okay, but I'm not standing outside someone's house while you enjoy your life as Irving High's starting quarterback."

Several minutes later, the Toyota pickup slowed as it approached Highway 114. Seeing an eighteen-wheeler coming, Craig hit the accelerator to beat it. His tires spun out on the loose gravel, dangerously sending the pickup a few feet onto the highway. The eighteen-wheeler swerved, just missing them. Its loud horn blasted through the night.

Ray glanced at his buddy. "Do you have a death wish?"

"No. But at least this time, I would've been the one to get it first."

"And how does that help me? It was an eighteen-wheeler!"

The pickup continued on without incident, easing to a stop just outside a north Irving gated community. Seeing the guardhouse occupied at the main entrance, Craig slapped the steering wheel. "Now what?"

"Follow me," Ray replied, hopping out of the truck.

In the darkness, the two boys reached a six-foot-high stone wall and easily scaled it, landing on their feet on the other side.

"That was easy," Craig said. "I hope you know where you're going."

"I do. Just listen for the music and look for the cars."

A grassy median turned into a street, and soon the boys were jogging through the subdivision. When they found the house, cars lined the street and loud music floated over the roof.

"Come on," Ray said. "Let's go through the side gate."

Susan Hatfield had invited all her drill team members for a party. That's why the two Irving High School football players found the backyard full of girls. It was truly party time.

Somewhere after two in the morning, Craig tapped Ray on the shoulder. "Hey, buddy, we need to get back to the lake."

"Yeah, the party's winding down anyway. And I'm getting tired."

"For sure. You ran your butt off at the game."

"And I've been up since six," Ray said.

"Me too. Let's go."

They walked back out, jumping the fence in the same place and finding the pickup still there. Minutes later, they were headed back to the lake.

"Hey," Craig said, tapping his fuel gauge. "I need to stop and get some gas. Do you need anything?"

"Yeah," Ray mumbled. "Some sleep."

"Let me fill up and we'll be rolling."

Craig walked into the store and gave the clerk ten dollars for gas. When he'd finished pumping, he slid behind the wheel and found Ray fast asleep. "I wish I could join you," he whispered as he started up the car.

The trip took twenty minutes, the pickup truck rambling down Highway 114. It was near three a.m. and traffic was almost nonexistent. This section of highway was not heavily traveled, even during rush hour. For Craig, the yellow stripes raced by. Expansion joints in the road added to the soothing noise as the tires rolled over them creating a rhythmic beat. Earlier in the night, Craig had popped up the sunroof, allowing the cool breeze to envelop the cab. The combination of sound and air sent his head rolling side to side. It didn't take long before his heavy eyelids started to close.

The Toyota pickup drifted to the right, heading for a deep ditch. As the vehicle hit the edge of the shoulder, Craig opened his eyes and saw the coming disaster. With only one move, he swerved to the left, sending the pickup into a roll. Wearing his seatbelt, he had a front row seat as Ray's body broke through the sunroof face first, flying through the air into the deep night. After several full rolls, the pickup came to rest.

Craig wiped his face clear of broken glass, his left arm half-buried in some field. The pickup was on its side. The smell of gas and oil and antifreeze wafted into the cab through the smashed windshield. It took a minute, but Craig regained his senses and realized he needed to get out of the truck. Fast!

Scrambling up through Ray's empty seat, he swung the door open and climbed on top of the pickup. Scanning the darkness, he didn't see Ray. This was bad.

He touched the underside of the truck and burned his hand. With no choice, he jumped down, thankful his two legs weren't broken. As soon as he hit the dirt, he started calling out. "Ray! Ray! Where are you?"

With the truck lights out, he couldn't see anything. All he could do was feel his way, hoping to run into Ray… or his body.

Craig fought back tears as the ramifications of this nightmare hit him. He searched frantically, scrambling around on his knees and feeling with his hands through whatever crops the farmer had planted. And he never stopped calling out his good friend's name. "Ray! Ray! Please, where are you?"

In the distance, a pair of headlights sliced through the darkness. This gave Craig a chance to see more of the scene. As the headlights came nearer, he realized he was still in the field and not near the road. Oblivious as to how close the headlights were, he kept searching.

Suddenly, he heard air brakes engage and tires squeal. Spinning to his right, he saw an eighteen-wheeler skidding on Highway 114. When it stopped, Craig staggered through the ditch and shoulder, ending up in front of its grille. There, against the dark asphalt, he found a sack of clothes soaked in red. Tiny rivers of blood trickled down the highway.

It was Ray.

Chapter Two

Everything was quiet.

Maria Cerda repositioned herself across the narrow bed, fluffing up a pillow before laying her head down again with a sigh. Her husband worked the night shift at the post office, which meant she had the bed to herself until he got back. The window unit kicked on again, humming quietly, lulling her back to sleep as it blew cold air into the small room.

She let her eyes close once more, floating between dreams and reality. Just as she was about to give in to sleep entirely, a loud noise echoed down the hallway.

Maria lifted her head, scanning the empty room with a frown. Then she heard it again—knocking. Hard. Loud. Her pulse quickened.

Swinging her legs off the bed, she found her slippers and wrapped a robe around her shoulders as she made her way down the dark hall. Reaching the living room, she switched on a lamp. By now, she could feel the vein in her neck throbbing. With her husband gone and her son at the lake, any knock at this time could not be good news. She took a deep breath as she undid the locks and flipped on the porch light.

The door slowly swung open to reveal an Irving police officer. Hands shaking, Maria pushed the screen door toward the officer. "Please come in," she said. "Our doorbell doesn't work."

Saying nothing, the officer stepped into the living room.

"What is it?" Maria asked, her eyes glistening over.

"Do you have a son named Ray Cerda?"

"Yes," Maria managed.

"He's been in an accident," the officer said coldly. "He's in serious condition at the HEB Hospital."

"Oh God!" she screamed. Her knees buckled, forcing her to fall back in a chair.

The officer pulled out his notepad. "Ma'am, is your husband home?"

She shook her head, unable to find words.

"Do you know how to reach him?"

Sobbing, she nodded.

Debbie appeared in the hallway, eyes widening at the sight of Maria and the police officer. Behind her was Ninfa, a live-in cook/maid/babysitter from Mexico. The scream had woken the pair.

"Mom, w-what's happened?" Debbie asked.

"It's Ray, Jr.!" she cried. "He's been in an accident."

Debbie covered her mouth as she went to Ninfa for comfort. The officer kept his eyes on his notepad, his mouth set in a grim line as the three women sobbed together. When thirteen-year-old David staggered out from his bedroom, the officer spoke up. "Ma'am, do you want me to drive you to the hospital, or can you get your husband to do that?"

Maria tried her best to draw air into her lungs. "I'll call my husband. He'll take us."

The officer tipped his hat and exited through the front door, disappearing into the darkness.

Ray, Sr. ran every red light on the way to the hospital. There wasn't any traffic, so it didn't matter. Maria sat next to him, with Debbie and Ninfa in the backseat. Tears dotted all four faces, each one fearful of what they were about to see.

Spotting the emergency room, Ray, Sr. screeched his car to a stop and made sure everyone was out before jogging to the check-in desk.

"I'm Ray Cerda, Sr. My son Ray Cerda, Jr., is he here?"

The woman nodded and flipped through a list. "Please wait over there and I'll have the doctor come and talk to you."

"Is he okay?" Ray, Sr. asked frantically.

"I don't know," the woman replied. "All I can say is that he's here."

Ray, Sr. persisted. "What kind of accident was he in?"

"Again, sir, I don't know. Please, the doctor will be out shortly."

Ray, Sr. clenched his fists, not moving from his spot. Finally, he went over to his wife and relayed what he knew. The four sat there, dabbing their eyes and staring at nothing.

Twenty minutes later, a doctor with a clipboard appeared. "Mr. Ray Cerda?"

"That's me," Ray, Sr. said, springing from the chair and bringing Maria, Debbie, and Ninfa in his wake. "How is my son?"

The doctor led the group to an empty hallway. "First, I want to say he's been badly injured. According to the paramedics, the truck he was in rolled several times, ejecting him through the windshield or sunroof."

Maria moaned and clung to her husband. The doctor let that sink in before continuing. "That leads me to the next part: We can't be sure he will survive this. We're doing all we can, but he needs facilities and equipment we don't have. So we're transferring him to another hospital."

Ray, Sr. and the three women were crying again. Ray, Sr. collected himself enough to speak. "Well, do it right away!"

"Can we see him?" Maria asked before the doctor disappeared.

"We've cleaned him up and stabilized him. He's not conscious, but I'll let you see him briefly." The doctor put a hand on Ray, Sr.'s shoulder. "However, I don't recommend it. He looks... not normal."

"I want to see my son," Maria demanded.

The doctor nodded and led the four through a maze until he reached a recovery area. There, lying on his back, was Ray.

"Oh my God!" Maria screamed. "Ray!"

Debbie grabbed her mother while Ray, Sr. leaned against a wall to steady himself. Ninfa walked closer to the injured boy before withdrawing in horror. What they saw was not Ray, Jr. It was a nightmare.

Gone was the beautiful baby-face of a sixteen-year-old athlete and honor student. In his place was a collection of skin, bone, and blood, haphazardly and partially assembled. His face, double in size, had deep gashes through his cheeks and forehead. A piece of his face flapped loosely around several tubes protruding from his nose and mouth. Every few seconds, a machine pumped air into his lungs. The scene belonged in a haunted house on Halloween, not a hospital bed.

Ninfa and Debbie left the room, unable to look anymore. Maria's eyes lingered for a moment more before she followed them out. Only Ray, Sr. stayed, making sure the doctors understood the urgency of this matter. They did.

An hour later, an air ambulance whisked the young boy to St. Paul's Hospital near downtown Dallas. Before Ray, Sr. and his family could arrive, the skilled surgeons set to work. When the Cerda family entered, a nurse spoke to them briefly before letting them see Ray, Jr. again.

Maria was first and felt her heart stop when she saw a priest giving her son his last rites. Ray, Sr., Debbie, and Ninfa saw the priest and began crying again. Then they focused their attention on Ray, Jr.

He had gone from a corpse in a haunted house to an experiment by Dr. Frankenstein. A metal halo was screwed into his skull. Attached to it were twisted steel cables supporting thirty-five pounds of weights. These hung down, pulling his neck away from his spine. A large tube was stuck in his mouth. Below his head were straps holding down every part of his body. An IV came from his arm. White circles dotted his chest and arms, attached to various machines all beeping. Suddenly, the bed moved, causing the Cerdas to step back in fear.

"What's going on?" Maria asked the nurse.

"It's a Roto-Bed," he replied. "It tilts side to side to prevent respiratory issues, blood clots, and pressure sores. I know it looks strange, but it's vital to keeping your son alive."

They stood there, mouths open, as the bed rotated to the left, tilting Ray almost vertically on his side. Now they understood the need for the straps. The machine paused, then rotated to the right until he was vertical on his other side. This process repeated itself for at least a minute until the machine returned its cargo to the original level. With nothing moving, Ray's zombie eyes remained fixed on the ceiling.

Through the straps, halo, weights, and tubes, the Cerdas noticed the loose flap on his face had been stitched up and his smashed nose packed with gauze. Still, no one in the Cerda family felt like Ray would survive this. The situation was grim.

When they had seen enough, a surgeon appeared to discuss the boy's prognosis. "His neck is broken and his spinal cord is damaged. We can't be sure how bad everything is until the swelling goes down. We'll have to wait seventy-two hours and reassess. Then, if the swelling has progressed enough, we can operate on him and see what we can do."

"Will we be able to talk to him?" Maria asked.

"Not for several days. We're keeping him sedated. The pain would be unbearable, and we don't want him moving until we can do an assessment. We're doing everything we can for your son—but I have to tell you, he may not make it."

Maria drew in a sharp breath, turned away, and stepped into the hall with Ninfa behind her. The two women began to pray. When they finished, they looked up and saw students pouring into the halls. A security guard motioned the two women back to the waiting room, where the rest of the Cerda family joined them.

Out in the halls, each Irving high school was represented: Nimitz, MacArthur, and Irving. Girls cried on boys' shoulders. Parents stood around, dazed, imagining what it would be like if their child was in there. For the Cerdas, the crowd comforted them. Having others share their pain and grief made the experience barely bearable.

One of the multitude of visitors was Ray's girlfriend, Allison Taylor. The family had been keeping everyone out, but let her in. Allison's reaction was no different than theirs. After less than thirty seconds, she walked out certain Ray would die. She cried with the other students for a while before going home, closing her door, and burying her head in a pillow. The future she'd thought she had was gone. At sixteen, she'd have to watch her boyfriend be lowered into the ground.

———

Joyce Read sat in a pink Cadillac, poring over the day's orders. "Not bad," she said to herself. "Maybe I'll earn another vacation this year."

She opened her car door, grabbing her satchel and purse before heading up her driveway. As a Mary Kay Cosmetics saleswoman, she had to hit the streets every day to make her living. Tall, thin, and tan, she turned a lot of men's heads. But the ones she had to sell to were women, so she had to use her appearance as an example of how her client could look in the Mary Kay makeup. So far, her career had been stellar.

Joyce set her things on the kitchen counter and heard crying coming from the TV room. On a sofa, she found her daughter Betty Jo—BJ to her friends—with tears streaming down her red cheeks. "BJ, what in the world is wrong?"

BJ stopped for moment to speak. "It's Little Ray. He's been in a car accident and... Mom, he's real bad!" She let out a wail. "I want to go over to the hospital."

Joyce just stood there, absorbing this news. Then she snatched up her purse and keys and told her daughter to get moving. "We're going there right now!"

The scene hadn't changed when Joyce and BJ stepped off the elevator. It seemed like half of Irving High School filled the halls. There were distraught kids strung out everywhere. The pair hugged the ones they knew, crying with them and picking up what information they could.

One student seemed to be in the know. "Ray might not make it. And even if he does, he'll never walk again."

"Oh God!" Joyce said. "That's terrible."

She pushed her daughter through the crowd close to the room. They were prevented from going in, but Debbie and Maria thanked them for coming. With heavy hearts, they left.

On the drive home, Joyce's thoughts raced. *Little Ray is going to be our senior quarterback! He's finishing up his high school career, getting ready for college. And now, this? How can that be?!*

"Mom, do you think he's going to make it?"

"I don't know, honey, but St. Paul's has one of the best trauma units around. I'm sure he's in good hands. Let's just think positive. Okay?"

"But even if he does, he'll be in a wheelchair for the rest of his life."

Joyce bit her bottom lip. "Well, maybe there's something we can do to help."

"Like what?" BJ asked.

"There's got to be something. Just let Mom think. I'll come up with something."

●——●

It had been more than three days, but it felt like a lifetime for Maria. She had spent every night in the hospital, along with her husband. Their only breaks were trips home to shower and grab fresh

24

clothes. Every meal was from the hospital cafeteria. With a steady stream of visitors who had to be kept out, one day bled into another.

By now, at least she knew the routine. The first day had been rough. Every time the bed had rotated, she'd jumped back. At one point, there had been a foul stench. She had pressed the button for the nurse, and the staff came in and cleaned up Ray's behind. The doctors told her that his body would keep pushing out the waste and they would clean it up. Since there was no way to know when that happened, they asked Maria and Ray, Sr. to call them when they smelled something.

Another awkward moment was seeing them change out Ray's catheter. It was one thing to see your son's genitals when he was a two-year-old. But sixteen? Maria, Ninfa, and Debbie learned to step out whenever the nurses were doing something like that.

At times, Maria wanted to reach over and touch her son's broken face. But the doctors told her not to. Moving the wrong part could be disastrous. They explained their top priority was keeping Ray stabilized so the swelling could go down. This was supposed to take seventy-two hours. Today, time was up.

"Mr. and Mrs. Cerda," the surgeon said. "We want to talk to you about your son's progress. I've invited Doctor Ninjab and Doctor Waring to attend this meeting. Is that okay?"

"Yes," Ray, Sr. said, pulling his heavy coat tight around his neck. "Can I ask you why it's freezing in this room?"

"Of course," the surgeon said. "There are several reasons. First, the cold air is good for his swelling. Hot temperatures would be bad. The second reason is moisture. For patients with your son's condition, lung problems can turn into pneumonia, which can lead to death. We need to keep moisture out of his lungs. Moisture also harbors bacteria. The air conditioning removes the moisture with cold air, much like a cold glass collecting water on the sides. The colder we can get it, the more moisture we remove. If you've ever seen water dripping from your window unit or a pipe coming from your attic, that's the condensate we're removing. Does that make sense?"

Ray, Sr. and Maria nodded.

"Good. The final reason is that patients with spinal breaks like your son lose the ability to sweat. The purpose of sweat is to carry the heat from below the skin to the surface, where it evaporates. Since Ray can't sweat, his body could overheat. That would be dangerous and possibly deadly."

Again, the Cerdas nodded.

"All right. We've met and studied the data and X-rays. We intend to operate on your son very soon. But first, we're going to bring him out of the sedation so we can perform a test on his feet and legs. This test involves poking needles into parts of his lower extremities. We need to see what he can feel. I don't want to get your hopes up, however. We believe he'll be paralyzed for the rest of his life. In fact, we believe he'll be a quadriplegic."

"Oh God, no!" Maria said as she buried her head in her husband's shoulder.

"A quadriplegic?" Ray, Sr. said, trying his best to remain calm. By now, he'd cried so much he was out of tears. "Will he be able to use his arms?"

"We don't know. But after the test, if it goes the way we think it will go, we intend to tell him his situation."

Ray, Sr. grabbed the surgeon's arm. "Please don't! Not now. Let's wait until he gets out of the hospital."

The startled surgeon eased his arm from Ray, Sr.'s grasp. "I'm sorry, Mr. Cerda, but we can't do that. He has to know right now and begin to accept and deal with it. Trust me, this is for the best."

Ray, Sr. shook his head in disbelief. Maria lifted her head up to see her husband's expression before laying her head back down.

"Is there anything else we need to know?" Ray, Sr. asked.

"Yes. The surgery is very risky. He might not make it. We recommend having your priest in here when we test him. Then, right before we sedate him again, the priest can give the last rites."

●——●

It was close to eight on the morning of the fourth day when Maria pressed the button over and over again.

"Yes, what is it?" the ICU nurse asked.

"He's opening his eyes," Maria replied. "I think he's waking up."

The nurse left, returning with the surgeon. He studied Ray, using a tiny flashlight on his eyes. "Ray, can you hear me?" the surgeon said.

Ray's eyes flitted open, then shut. The surgeon leaned in closer. "Ray, can you hear me? Blink your eyes if you are awake."

Nothing.

The surgeon turned his gaze to Ray, Sr. and Maria, who were holding each other up. He shook his head.

Chapter Three

I tried to open my eyes, but it was hard. Very hard. The light was blinding.

"Hey, he's awake!" someone yelled. "Get the nurse."

Between the beeping and pinging sounds that surrounded me, I heard feet scuffling. Even though my eyes were closed, I sensed the lights dim. I took this chance to open them. What I saw frightened me. A man in black floated above my face, pointing his hand at me. He held a rosary.

It's a priest saying something I don't understand. This must be a dream. I'm going back to sleep...

I heard some people talking next to me. One of them was my mom. That comforted me. I struggled to lift my heavy eyelids, but the light still hurt too much. It felt like someone had put my head in a vise. I couldn't move anything.

"Look!" Mom said. "He's opening his eyes again. Debbie, get the nurse."

By opening and closing my eyes, I slowly adjusted to the bright lights. Yet I couldn't see anything but the ceiling directly above me. I tried to make my lips form words, but they wouldn't budge. Someone had shoved a tube down my throat, forcing me to breathe. I couldn't even use my nose because it was all blocked up.

What is this place? I just want to wake up from this nightmare.

My eyes fixed on the ceiling, studying the stipple in the white tiles. A few divots spoiled an otherwise clean surface. I thought about moving my head, but a tremendous weight was pulling my head away from my shoulders. I couldn't feel my hands or legs.

This is definitely the worst nightmare I've ever had. It's so real I'm actually scared.

Suddenly, the bed moved, rotating me to the right. There, I saw my parents with dark circles under their eyes, peering at me with frowns. The rotation stopped and started in the other direction, taking them out of my view. Now I saw different faces.

There's Chonny and Debbie and David. Where's Ninfa?

I rotated back and forth for several minutes. On my trips to the left, Debbie looked like she had been crying. Finally, Ninfa appeared. I could see the same dark circles under her eyes. I remembered when Debbie used to teach Ninfa English.

That reminds me, I have to finish a term paper for English and turn in some homework on Monday. I need to get out of this dream and get it done. I think I'll close my eyes and see if I can wake up.

"Ray, are you awake?"

I struggled to see who was talking to me.

"Blink your eyes if you hear me."

I blinked several times, taking a moment to adjust to the light. The temperature all around me was near freezing.

Yeah, this must be hell.

"Can you see my face?" the voice asked.

I forced my eyes open long enough to see a strange man leaning over me.

"I've taken the breathing tube out of your mouth. If you can't talk, just blink your eyes twice if you see my face."

I croaked out a hoarse reply.

"Good. It will take a little bit to regain your voice. I'm Doctor Laird and you are at St. Paul's Hospital in Dallas. You've been in a car accident. Do you understand me?"

Car accident? Dallas? I live in Irving.

"Ray, do you understand me? You've been in a car accident."

Dr. Laird's face drifted out of view as he straightened. "I don't think he understands. Where was his accident?"

"On Highway 114," my dad replied. I couldn't see him, but I recognized his voice. "He was supposed to be at Lake Grapevine with the other football players."

The lake! Yeah, I was hanging out there with the guys.

"But he left and went to a party in town. The accident happened when they were on the way back to the lake. I never should've let him go." I could hear deep guilt in Dad's voice.

Dr. Laird's face reappeared above me. "Ray, do you remember going to the lake with your fellow football players?"

Wait a minute! I was riding with Craig.

"Yes," I coughed out.

"Good." He turned his head. "I think we're reaching him." Facing me again, Dr. Laird continued. "Now, listen. You were a passenger in a car that was in an accident. Do you understand me?"

"Yes," I managed.

"Okay. You have broken some bones, including your spine. We need to perform some tests on you. All you have to do is stare up at the mirror we're going to place over you. Do you think you can do that?"

"Yes," I said again, my dry throat keeping me from saying anything more.

"Sandy," Dr. Laird said, "get him some ice chips."

A nurse leaned over to spoon a few ice chips into my mouth. They felt good sliding down my throat. A minute later, she held up a straw so I could drink some water.

"Thanks," I told her, my throat feeling better.

A mirror soon floated above me, connected to two sets of arms on each side of my bed. I couldn't see their faces, but assumed they were female nurses. The mirror tilted so I could see the end of the bed.

"Turn off the Roto-Bed," Dr. Laird ordered. "I don't want it rotating while we're doing this test."

He moved between the mirror and the end of my bed. "Ray, I'm going to lift the blanket and sheets off your feet. I'm going to be very careful."

I watched as he exposed the tops of my feet—the same feet that had set track records.

"Get this mirror behind his feet," Dr. Laird said. A nurse repositioned it. "Ray, can you see the bottom of this foot?"

"Yes," I replied. "I can see you touching it."

"Can you *feel* me touching it?"

"N-no."

"Okay, I'm going to stick a needle in your big toe. Let me know when you feel it." I watched as he made a jabbing move. "Do you feel this?" he asked in a stern voice.

"Feel what?" I said, unable to see if the needle was in my big toe.

He moved to another toe. "Do you see me sticking the needle in your second toe?"

"Yes."

"Do you feel it?"

"No."

It was this exact moment that I knew I was in deep, as in bottomless-pit deep, trouble.

Dr. Laird continued sticking every toe and I stopped responding. I felt nothing but fear—a gnawing, gripping sensation that had settled over my brain. When the nurses removed the mirrors, one of them accidentally gave me a brief glimpse of my mom. Her hands covered her face in despair as my dad hugged her. *They know I'm in trouble too.*

Dr. Laird came next to my face and leaned over. "Ray, the car accident broke your neck. You have severe damage to your spinal cord. It's what we call a C5-C6 break. We're going to prepare you for surgery to see if we can fuse your neck and repair and stabilize some of the damage. But I want you to understand that you will likely never walk again."

I closed my eyes, not wanting to hear any more. Yet he continued.

"Ray, the procedure we're going to perform is risky. You may die during the surgery or after it. Your parents have given consent for this surgery. But if you don't want it, I won't do it. Do you want me to go ahead with the surgery?"

I don't remember saying yes. The next thing I knew, the bed was rotating me again like a chicken on a rotisserie grill. Distraught faces on the left. Devastated family on the right.

I need to get out of here and finish up the school year. I have too many things to do this summer. I know this has to be a dream. If I close my eyes, I'll wake up any minute. Then I'll have a good chuckle at how scary it was.

"Ray, it's me, Allison."

I opened my eyes to see my precious girlfriend. Her eyes looked like Mom's and Ninfa's.

"Allison," I said before the bed started rotating. When it turned back toward her, my eyes were forced to see her face, then her chest and entire body—slender and athletic—all the way down to her knees. A quick pause and I tracked back up to her face before heading to the other side. It was maddening seeing someone for a brief moment like this. She was talking about me getting out of here so we could do all the things we'd planned. I couldn't see how that would happen now, but I played along and tried to act positive.

I don't remember her leaving—just that I saw Kyle, my childhood friend, next. He wore a big smile, but it looked fake. In fact, he looked worse than my family.

"Ray, Coach Hamberger and Coach Stalcup have been out in the hall with everyone from Irving High. There's so many other students here it's incredible. We're all pulling for you, buddy," he said in an upbeat tone. But I could tell that as soon as I rotated away, he'd be out in the hall crying with the rest of them.

A few more friends and teammates came in, each one freaking out when they saw me. They desperately tried not to, but they couldn't help it. We all knew they were attending a funeral and viewing a body in an open casket. It was surreal. All I needed was a tux with a rose in the lapel.

When a nurse came back, she shooed everyone out and injected something into my IV line. Then everything disappeared.

Time had no meaning, no length, no starting or stopping point. I was trapped in a wormhole in space where everything including time disappeared—only to reappear somewhere else, very far away.

I awoke to the bed shaking, still struggling to get my eyes open. When I did, I saw several male orderlies removing parts from my bed. Hovering over me was that man in black again, waving a cross over my face and speaking words from another language.

Once they were done, I was wheeled down a long hall. Mom leaned over from one side and Dad from the other. They had the look of parents who were never going to see their child again. Before I could panic, I passed out.

●—●

Cold.

Freezing cold.

That's all I felt physically, lying there with my eyes closed among all the beeping.

Lonely.

Afraid.

Confused.

That's what I felt emotionally. I tried to change my mind, to think positive. I thought about football, and my upcoming season as the starting quarterback. My girlfriend. My teammates. My family. Then I grew afraid again.

Through all the sedation, I hovered between consciousness and nothingness. I had no idea how many days I'd been here.

"Ray, we're going to do another test." It was Dr. Laird again, appearing out of the thin, cold air. I couldn't wait until I never heard his voice again.

They set up the mirrors so I could see the doctor jam a needle into all ten toes. Just to make sure, he stuck my arch and heel. I felt nothing.

When they had cleared everything away, he came up to my face and gave me the news. "Ray, the surgery was successful. We fused your neck to prevent the spinal cord from further damage. But my initial assessment has not changed. You will not walk again, nor have any feeling in your legs. You may have some feeling in your chest, but how high up, it's hard to tell. We've done all we can for you here. Today is Sunday. They will likely come for you tomorrow and move you to a rehabilitation clinic. You'll be there for four to six months."

"So... so I was at the lake Friday. If today's Sunday, I've been here two days?"

"Uh, no. Eight days. A week has passed since you were brought here."

I had been in a low place when they'd first stuck me with the needles. I'd known I was in trouble. But now—hearing that a successful surgery meant I'd never walk again or have feeling up to who knows where—this was so much lower. And the fact that I wouldn't be going home, but instead to some strange place? I couldn't even process it. I just let the sedation take me away until I was better equipped to deal with my new future.

———•

The ICU room lacked windows, so I had no sense of what time it was when the men came for me.

"Ray, we're going to roll you to the elevator and take you downstairs to an ambulance. Okay?"

"Yeah," I said, staring at the ceiling. "Are my parents here?"

"I don't see anyone."

"What time is it?" I asked the unseen face.

"Eight thirty."

"At night or the morning?"

"At night."

"What day is this?"

"Monday."

Monday. I closed my eyes as the men did their thing. My parents had missed so much work they could have been fired. Dad was probably working extra shifts to make up for the ones he'd missed. Besides taking care of David, Mom worked as a collector for Citigroup. She was probably doing the same as Dad and working overtime to make up for a week of lost time. Even if they both had sick time they could use, we needed the money. We were a working-class family. All of us worked hard for everything. No one handed us anything.

My journey to the ambulance was a series of new ceilings down a long hall, different than the one I'd been rolled down to surgery. I got to see the elevator's ceiling and the seams hiding the escape hatch they always show in the movies. The emergency room's lobby was next—nothing special. Then I studied the ceiling of the covered porch where ambulances picked up and dropped off patients. Last was the metal of the ambulance's interior ceiling. I guessed it had been wiped down and sanitized a thousand times.

"You doing okay?" one of the unseen attendants asked as he closed the rear doors.

"Yeah." What else could I say?

With nothing to do, I lay there listening to the two attendants talk.

"Hey, Charlie, did you see the Ranger game? Sample knocked two homers off the Royals. Rangers killed 'em."

"Yeah, they can turn it on when they want. But they still suck. Zimmer's going to get fired. You'll see."

"Maybe, but I'm heading out there before it gets too hot. You wanna come?"

"Nah. I'm repainting the bedroom for Marcy. She's been on my ass for months. If I don't get it done, I'll come home one day and the locks will be changed."

"I thought the house was in your name."

"It is. That's how bad I need to get the room painted."

They went on and on about beer, work, and TV shows. I was a mere package being delivered to someone's front door. To make the ride worse, I tasted antiseptic with each swallow. During the last surgery, the doctors had reset my broken nose, packing medicated gauze up each nostril. If I swallowed real hard, I could almost feel a piece of gauze hanging down the back of my throat, threatening to gag me. It was yet another misery to add to this unbelievable catastrophe.

Darkness filled the ambulance. I had noticed it briefly when they'd loaded me up. I hoped because the evening was getting on, Mom and Dad would be waiting to greet me at this new place. If not both, maybe one of them.

The ride was uneventful and relatively smooth. Throughout this transfer, I never saw the complete face of any of the attendants—just a sideburn here and a chin there.

The ambulance came to a stop, then backed up. When it stopped again, I heard one of the attendants open the rear doors and hop out.

"We're here, buddy," the attendant said.

As they pulled me out, I had no idea where *here* was. I couldn't see the front of the building or even the roof. My only view was a dark sky with low clouds. An ominous beginning for sure.

They rolled me in, receiving directions from unseen voices on the intercom. When they opened two large doors, I felt the freezing cold air again. I had missed enjoying the warm outdoors from the hospital to the ambulance to here. I wished I would've soaked in more of the May air. *How long will it be before I can go outside again?* I wondered.

"Okay, buddy, we're done," the attendant said after he and several others carefully transferred me to another bed, maintaining the thirty-five-pound weight pulling my skull from my body. "You're in Room Five, and it looks like you have plenty of company. Good luck to you."

From the edges of my vision, I saw a plastic curtain pulled around my bed. A young girl leaned over my face. "Ray Cerda, I'm Gia Renatta. I'm your nurse until midnight. I'm just going to set your bed to start rotating. You had one of these in the hospital, right?"

"Yeah. Are my parents here?" I asked, trying to hide my desperation.

"I don't know," she replied. "But I'll check. In the meantime, you relax as I hook everything up."

She plugged in my IV and several other monitors before straightening up my blanket. When I heard the curtain slide back and close, I assumed she was gone.

"Hey, I need more pain meds!" a man yelled. "Come on! You do this to me each night."

I heard footsteps, a curtain slide, and a woman's hushed voice. I couldn't see anything other than the dirty white tiles above me. Then I made my first roll.

When I'd first experienced the rotating bed in the hospital, it'd been a form of torture. As Mom would talk to me, I'd leave her. To see more of me, she would crouch down when the bed came back to her. It also disturbed my sleep. There was no way to get any more than fifteen minutes of unbroken sleep. But now, I'd finally found one positive aspect of the Roto-Bed: I could see the world around me. And what I saw was alarming.

On my turn to the right, I spotted another bed like mine just underneath the curtain. I wondered who was in it.

When I rolled to the left, a gap in the curtain let me see an arm and shoulder of a real person, again in a bed like mine. I studied everything I could before I rolled away. It was like taking snapshots in your mind so you could examine them later. All I wanted to do was understand what this place was.

I finally stopped rotating and assessed my situation. I was freezing again, wishing I had told the nurse to pull the covers up to my chin. Unable to breathe through my nose, I had to sense smells through my mouth. Out of nowhere, an unhuman stench hit my tongue.

"Hey, come clean this shit up!" a voice yelled. It was the same one that had complained about the pain meds. "Billy shit himself again. Oh God, and this one reeks."

He was right about the reeking part. I didn't even have the use of my nose and it was terrible. Like tasting rat poison.

A minute passed until I heard footsteps and the curtain to my left slide back.

"Get the wipes," a woman said. "We're going to need to wash him up."

I started rotating again, first to my right. Nothing had changed there. Then to the left. The nurses had accidentally increased the gap in my curtain, so I could see them working. When I made the second rotation, the man's bed started rotating. This let me see his genitals. A clear tube protruded from his penis. Underneath that, a dark mess oozed between his legs. For brief second, we locked eyes. He had been watching me studying him. Before we rotated away from each other, I could see a distant, faraway look in his eyes. It didn't seem like he even cared.

"Gia, stop his bed from rotating," one of the nurses ordered. "Always do that *before* we start cleaning them up."

They eventually finished up with him and left. For a moment, everything was quiet. Then I heard something from the right. It was soft at first, but unmistakable. Yes, a man was crying.

"Hey, Rodeo Man," the same angry voice yelled. "I can hear you crying from all the way over here. Stop that shit!"

He didn't stop. It grew more intense.

What is this place? I thought to myself. *A nuthouse? Is that where I am? And where's my parents?*

I heard the bed to my right start rotating. The sobbing grew louder when he rotated toward me and less when he spun away. Back and forth this went until the bed stopped. It was then that I raced past "afraid" and took up residence in "terrified."

M inutes or maybe hours later, my curtains pulled back and Nurse Gia appeared. "How are you doing?"

"Did you see my parents?" I asked, desperate for some good news.

"No, I'm afraid I saw no one out there."

I felt my lips quiver. "I-I don't want to be here," I said, my voice trembling.

She leaned over and smiled. "How old are you?"

"Sixteen."

"Don't worry," she said in a comforting voice, "things will work out. You'll feel better in the morning." She leaned away from me, out of sight.

"Wait!" I said. "Please don't go. Can't you stay here and talk to me?"

"I can't," she replied, unseen. "I have to check on other patients. But I'll check on you a little later. Why don't you try to get some sleep?"

Sleep is the last thing I want, I thought to myself as she closed the curtain and abandoned me.

I stared at the ceiling, thinking about where I was and how my life would be different now. Deep, terrifying, indescribable thoughts filled my mind. I wanted some help, but couldn't even press a button to summon a nurse. I was truly all alone.

I felt something on the right side of my cheek. Then I felt it on the left side. That's when I realized they were tears. I was crying, just like the man next to me. And the worst part was, I couldn't even move my arms to wipe my face.

"Mom, where are you?" I sobbed to myself. "I just want to go home."

Chapter Four

It was the longest night of my life. I was so scared, I didn't fall asleep. I kept thinking my parents would come and make it all right, but they didn't.

A light filtered in through the windows, allowing me to see more details on the ceiling tiles. As I lay there, I heard the other patients in my room stirring. Of course, the hum of the rotating beds never let up. To make things worse, the beds weren't timed for exactly fifteen minutes. The bed on my right seemed to gain a minute or more each hour. Or my bed was slower by thirty seconds. It was hard to tell. Either way, I synced up with him after fourteen hours. I synced up with the guy on my right after twenty hours. It was impossible to be sure because I wasn't wearing a watch, and couldn't lift my arm even if I was. When I wasn't crying or completely freaking out, these were the kinds of observations I made—bed rotation synchronicity. How the other patients survived this I had no idea.

With antiseptic constantly draining down the back of my throat and the room so cold I could almost see my breath, I remained completely immobile, praying for a miracle. I decided my best course was to live minute by minute. By focusing on the next rotation or the next noise, I kept my mind from venturing into dark territory. I did not want to be in dark territory, because intense fear was there to greet me. Believe me, it wasn't pretty.

The only thing I looked forward to—the moment I desperately clung to—was a nurse pulling back my curtain to check my IV. Sometimes she adjusted the monitor or pulled my blanket up, even if I didn't ask. She was no mother, but she was a living, breathing human being who at least seemed to care. For prisoners in solitary confinement with no human contact, I could understand how they wasted away. I remembered the story from my history book about a medieval king who wanted to know the language God had given to Adam and Eve. After thinking about it, he decided to take a group of babies from their mothers before they had heard one word of any language. The midwives delivering them were told to say nothing. And the nurses caring for the babies could only feed and bathe them. No words or sounds at all.

The king never learned God's language, but he did make an unexpected discovery: Babies die without basic contact or interaction. They needed affection, warmth, and mainly love. Not one baby survived. If I hadn't before, I totally believed that story now.

Between waiting for rotations, I spent my hours counting the tiny divots in the ceiling tiles. I could never get the same number twice.

Two rotations after first light, a roadkill-like stench hit my mouth. I tried holding my breath, but couldn't for very long. I had to live.

"Hey! Hey!" the angry man yelled. "The new kid shit himself. Get in here now and wipe his ass down!"

He was right. There was no way around it. I had messed myself. The realization that I'd be lying here, unable to move and crapping myself at random times for the rest of my life, was unbearable. Just when I'd thought I couldn't go lower, I'd found there was another set of stairs headed down to a place that grew darker and darker with each step. Then the nurses appeared, and it was time to go even lower.

Using some straps under my legs, they carefully lifted them up and pulled out a fabric protector that had been put down for just such a purpose. Even though I couldn't feel it, one nurse stood on my right side, clearly handling my genitals. Seeing the panic in my eyes, she said, "I'm adjusting your catheter."

I closed my eyes, embarrassed to think of a woman touching me that way.

"Lift those up so I can clean underneath them," the other nurse ordered.

I knew she was talking about my balls. *I'm only sixteen, for crying out loud. This shouldn't be happening.* I just kept my eyes closed because I didn't want to see their expressions.

They worked efficiently, no doubt unwilling to breathe in my stink longer than absolutely necessary. I could taste the powder they spread between my butt cheeks and private parts. I remembered seeing the same thing done to my brother David when he was a little baby. Now I was no different.

The nurses had been gone for a few minutes when Mom arrived. I was so grateful she'd missed my bowel movement and nudity that my excitement to see her multiplied exponentially.

"Ray," she said, kissing my forehead, "I'm so sorry. We went to the hospital last night and found out you were transferred. By the time we made it here, it was after nine and they had locked the place down. I'm so sorry, honey. Your father will come by tonight and see you. I'll try to come back, but we have both missed so much work."

Hearing this, I began to understand the guilt my parents were feeling. They were trying to pay the bills to keep our house and cars running. But they were also trying to see me. Sometimes they couldn't do both. And since I wasn't going anywhere, well…

"How are you doing?" she asked.

"I just want to go home," I said with a level of desperation I didn't think possible. I really meant it.

"I know, sweetheart, but you have to get better here. They're going to get you well enough to come home. Just follow their instructions."

We talked for another ten minutes about my brothers, Chonny and David, and my sister, Debbie. She told me how Ninfa was praying, and all the students wished me well. She hovered over me so I could see her, then pulled away suddenly whenever her eyes filled up. She was probably grateful for the setup, because she could hide her devastated expressions from me unless I started rotating. I was programmed to first rotate to the right. That's why I noticed her standing on my left. If she was quietly sobbing out of my vision, she wouldn't be busted when the bed began rotating. She would have some time before I could rotate to the left and see her face.

Mom said goodbye way too soon and left me there alone. I was pretty sure she cried all the way back to the car. I know I did when I heard her soft footsteps disappear through the double doors.

"Nurse, could you wipe his eyes, please?" I heard a man's voice at the foot of my bed.

A young girl with a smooth cotton rag leaned over and wiped my face. I was focused on not crying when the bed tilted, lowering my legs and raising my head enough to see a group of people standing there.

"Hello, I'm Dr. Cody," a man in a white coat said. "I'll be in charge of your rehabilitation. These three women are your therapists." He pointed to a woman on his left. "This is Christy Avalon. She's your physical therapist. This one here on my right is Sheri Jones, your occupational therapist. And finally, this one on the other side of Sheri is your respiratory therapist, Elena Ravich."

Dr. Cody lifted my sheet, exposing my genitals. "Good. Your indwelling catheter is doing fine." He turned to another nurse in the background. "Note the output," he said. Then he turned back to me. "Ray, this bag helps us measure how much urine you produce each day. It tells us that your kidneys are working just fine."

"Okay," I said, silently urging him to put the sheet back down, especially with these three women looking on, comparing me with the other patients.

Dr. Cody released the sheet and flipped some pages on a clipboard. "When the swelling in your face goes down, we have you scheduled for plastic surgery. That will be in a week or two. I'll let you know when that's coming up."

"Okay," I said again.

"Now," he said, clearing his throat, "I need to explain some things. You have broken your vertebrae and severed your spinal cord at the C5-6 break. Your spinal cord is a long, thin, tubular bundle of nerve tissue. Think of it as an electrical cable. It transfers communications from your brain down to your body. Everything that's connected below the break can't communicate with your brain. That's why you have no feeling in your legs and lower body. Your vertebrae have one job: to protect the spinal cord. If you had broken your vertebrae but not severed your spinal cord, you'd be walking. So it's your spinal cord that's the key. Today, we don't have the technology to repair a spinal cord. All we can do is teach you how to use what tools you have left. And teach you we shall. I understand you're an athlete?"

"Yeah," I replied, not happy with the information he was giving me.

"Good. Because we will be harnessing the same training techniques and goals athletes use. We'll be working you hard, expecting you to give your best. Are you up to it?"

"Yes," I replied, unable to think of a better answer.

"Okay, good. Any questions?"

"Why is it so cold?"

Dr. Cody pointed to a vent in the ceiling. "The cold air reduces the moisture, which could hurt your lungs and grow bad things around the clinic. We don't want that. Plus, folks with your condition don't sweat, which is how the body eliminates heat."

I wasn't sure I'd heard that right. "Are you saying I'll never sweat again?"

"That's correct. You'll have to be very careful not to get overheated, since your body won't be able to properly cool itself down."

Oh man, this just keeps getting worse.

"When can I get this gauze out of my nose?" I asked.

"Probably Friday."

"What's today?"

"Tuesday."

"How long will I be here?"

"Four months—*at least.*"

I closed my eyes, fighting back the tears. More surgery. Never sweating again. Random craps. *I don't think I can do this.*

•——•

"Hello, Ray," a voice said as I heard the curtain slide back. "I'm Elena Ravich, your respiratory therapist. I met you earlier?"

"Oh yeah," I said as she came into view.

"My job is simple. I have to clear your lungs of fluid and make sure they get big and strong. Let's get started."

She inserted a plastic tube and told me to blow until a little ball inside reached the top. I thought it would be easy, but it wasn't. Between the massive amounts of sedation I had received and the effects of being a quadriplegic, I couldn't make the tiny ball hit the top.

"That's okay," she said. "It takes time. Let's try it again."

This went on for ten to fifteen minutes, and all I could do was lift the ball up a short way. My first venture into rehab was a complete bust.

I was feeling sorry for myself when I heard something to my right. "Don't worry, Ray. I'm just here to visit your neighbor," a man's voice said.

"Who are you?" I asked, unable to see him.

"I'm Andy Wortham. The guys in here call me State Farmer."

"Why?" I asked.

"I sell insurance. Or at least, I used to."

"Are you a patient?" I asked the unseen voice.

"Yes. I've been here three months. They've finally got me into a wheelchair. With my limited arm movement, I can get around okay."

This was my chance to get some information. "How many patients are in here?"

"Six. Three on each side of the room. You have the middle bed. This guy on your right is Rodeo Man. He was injured riding a bull during a rodeo contest."

"Hey," I heard Rodeo Man say from his bed.

State Farmer continued. "The guy on your left is Rockstar. He played guitar in a band but was in a car accident. The guy directly across from you is Wal-Manager. He slipped on a wet bathroom floor and broke his back. And the guy cattycorner to your left is Closed Casket. He had a motorcycle accident and his family was planning his funeral when the docs saved him."

"Is that why he's angry all the time?" I whispered.

"No," he whispered back. "He's angry because he's not going back to the life he had—free and easy, and without consequence."

A women's voice from Rodeo Man's area interrupted us.

"Sorry," State Farmer said, "the nurses are done. I'm going to visit with him for a little bit. I'll see if I can check on you later."

"Wait! How did you get injured?"

"I was out jogging and a heavy tree branch fell on me. Never saw it coming."

Just then, my bed started spinning. As I rotated to my right, I noticed a shiny metal container on the back of State Farmer's wheelchair. I was puzzling over its purpose when I accidentally caught a glimpse of my face. It was the worst thing I'd ever seen. I didn't even recognize it. When the bed began rotating to the left, I closed my eyes and swore I wouldn't open them again until the bed completely stopped. But by the time it came around again, I couldn't stand it. I opened my eyes.

The stitches.

The nose.

The swelling.

The bruising.

A Hollywood makeup artist couldn't have done a better job. I now fully understood why everyone who had seen me freaked out. And I realized that back in the hospital, when the nurses had held the mirror over me, they had tilted it away so I couldn't see my face. Each time I didn't think I could go lower, I did.

How much farther down will I have to go?

•———•

The next day, my physical therapist showed up. She went over the things she'd be teaching me, like how to move the parts of my body that still worked and get stronger. When she discussed the process of getting into a wheelchair, memories of running track and flying past my competitors replayed in my mind. I couldn't fathom wheeling around in a wheelchair for the rest of my life.

Once she was done, the occupational therapist, Sheri Jones, spent some time with me. It was her job to teach me how to eat, dress, and shower—to do the things we need to do each day to live and work. Right now, though, there was nothing I could do but lie there and listen.

After she was gone, I tried to get some sleep. I must have been dozing, because when I awoke, there were two doctors and a nurse holding my bedsheet up, gazing at my privates. I closed my eyes—really the only thing I had control over. I listened for them to go, happy as their sounds went quiet. Then I heard a familiar voice and tasted her perfume.

"Ray, are you awake?"

I opened my eyes to see Allison leaning over me. "Hey, thanks for coming." It was the best I could do.

"Of course," she said in her sweet voice. "The swelling has gone down on your face."

"Yeah, but not all of it."

"You'll be back to the cute class president I know and love."

I noticed she'd left out the part about being a starting quarterback. "I sure hope so," I said. "They're going to start working with me soon to get my strength back and teach me how to get up out of here."

"Oh, that's wonderful. Then we can do some of the things we planned this summer."

"For sure," I said, less confidently than her.

"I feel like I need a parka every time I come here. Why is it so cold?"

"To keep the germs down," I replied, not wanting to get into the details of me never sweating again. "So, what have you been up to?"

It was the absolute worst question I could ask, because I had to listen to all the things I wanted to be doing: going to the movies, working at a job, attending parties, working out at the track and gym, and visiting relatives. I was truly grateful for her visiting me, but it was like being stuck in a hotel room just outside Disneyland while your friend tells you all the rides they rode. There was nothing I could do but imagine what it was like. I felt my life wasting away.

Allison finally left, only to be replaced by both of my parents. Dad was barely holding it in. The man of the family is supposed to be the tough guy, the protector. Yet it looked like Dad could crack at any moment. I'm sure my rotations gave him time to get himself together. It was rough, seeing him like that.

When visiting hours were over, I was alone, with nothing to break up the solitude except to listen to Open Casket—aka Angry Man—yell for something. It was dark outside when I heard something to my right.

"Hey, Ray, it's me again," State Farmer said. "You hanging in there?"

"I don't have much choice," I replied, much too harshly.

"Yeah, I hear you."

We stayed silent for a few minutes.

"How do you deal with this?" I finally asked.

"That's a good question. I really don't know. I mean, I thought about suicide, but I can't even roll myself to an overpass to jump off. When you lose the ability to kill yourself, you've really lost all control."

I was near tears. "I can't even control my crap. I can't hold a job, go to class—nothing. How can I live any kind of life when I'm shitting everywhere?"

"For that, at least, I have good news. They program you to crap."

"What? How is that possible?"

"My Uncle Willis lives in Arkansas near the Arkansas River. Once a month, he goes to the river and wades to a spot near the bank. He uses his hands to find a bed the catfish have cleared out. Then he'll wiggle his finger like a worm, waiting for a catfish to bite on it. When it does, he uses the rest of his fingers to grab the mouth and bring it to the surface. Sometimes they get so big—like forty pounds—that he has to use two hands. Uncle Willis calls it noodling. It's a southern thing."

"What does that have to do with me crapping?"

"The nurses will set up a program for you. It might be each night before you go to bed. Then they'll come in and stick their index finger up you and noodle the poop right out."

"You're joking," I said.

"No. You won't feel them noodling, but your bowel will, and it'll let loose of that catfish you ate earlier in the day. So, when you go to sleep tonight, just know that you'll be able to go places without worrying about crapping yourself. You'll just need to find someone to do your noodling."

When State Farmer left, I thought about what he'd said. My previous worry of crapping myself at an inopportune moment had turned into the new worry of finding someone to noodle me. Instead of catching a forty-pound catfish, they'd receive a two-foot stinky anaconda as their reward. I desperately hoped he was pranking me, because the reality of all this was too maddening. Now, all I had to do was try to get some sleep before the next rotation.

Or unexpected poop arrived.

Chapter Five

I t had been two weeks since I'd been in rehab. I looked back at those fourteen days and wanted to shake my head, but I couldn't because I was in a neck brace. Still, it had been a trying time.

I had celebrated the first Friday in rehab with a torture session. It was some time in the morning when a doctor appeared and said he was going to pull the gauze out of my nose. I told him fine, assuming it was a routine procedure. I mean, how much could soft cotton hurt? Turned out, a whole hell of a lot.

He stood over me with a pair of large tweezers and searched for the end. Finding it, he grabbed the gauze and slowly pulled it above my head. At about the second inch of gauze, shooting needles exploded inside my nose. The pain was staggering. I had no idea the inner linings were so sensitive.

As an athlete, I'd endured pain—but this was from another world. I begged him to stop. He did when the strip of bloody gauze grew to three feet above my head. Through tears and moaning, the doctor carefully draped the long red rope over the side of my bed and said, "We're almost done." Another two seconds of searing pain and it was over. I almost passed out. Yet now I was free to breathe. It felt wonderful. Then my world was rocked.

"Okay, Tiger," the doctor said. "We've got one nostril clear. Time for the second one."

"Are you kidding?" I asked, though I knew he wasn't. I could only breathe through my left nostril, so there had to be one still plugged up. I tried negotiating. "Any way you can come back later? You know, let me catch my breath?"

"No," he said cruelly. "You'd just dread it even more." With that, he latched the tweezers onto another piece of bloody gauze and pulled.

During the first nostril pull, I'd learned something interesting. When you've never experienced something, it can be scary because you don't know what to expect. However, once you've done it the first time, you know how bad it is. That makes the second round a thousand times worse. When he held the three-foot rope above my head, I knew he still had another two seconds' worth of torture to go. It was excruciating. If I'd been a secret agent, I would've given everything up.

I spent the rest of that Friday recuperating, enjoying a nice fresh meal of IV drip. It wasn't pretty, but this was my life.

●—●

Four days later, they carted me to the hospital for plastic surgery on my face. All I know is that I somehow made it back to rehab because I was lying there enjoying the sedation, not worried about the bandages or stitches in my head.

Until the drugs wore off.

Then it was back to mind-numbing pain. All I could think about was how much more I could take.

Several mornings and nights disappeared to who knows where when my physical therapist told me I was going to start sitting up. After getting the clearance from the doctor, she worked with me for ten minutes. Each time I tried to lift my head, I felt the blood rush to it—or from it, I have no idea which. I was so fatigued I nearly passed out cold. Every two hours she came back, trying to get me to sit up. "We have to build up your stamina and endurance," she said.

I had been an athlete with crazy hard workouts. Lifting my head and sitting up shouldn't have been that hard. But it was.

She brought a helper, and together they worked with me all day until they went home. I had made very little progress.

With my head on the pillow, I thought, *How in the world am I going to get through this?* That's when I spotted it. Someone had taped a poster to the ceiling above my bed. It said, "The road to success never ends." Below the saying was a long, straight road in the desert, with a man running on the yellow stripe. I considered the poster. The road to success may never end, but my ability to run has.

I was sure someone meant well, but seeing a guy running dropped me back down again. Fortunately, I now had a lot of visitors to keep me occupied. One of them was a relative, Joel Vela. He worked at Northlake College. Joel was relentless, doing his best to pump me up. I knew he was helping my family somehow, so I tried to be positive when he showed up.

Dave Portillo, a good high school friend and teammate, came by to cheer me up. Kyle and Allison came too. Then there was Joyce Read. The energetic redhead bounced in telling me she was going to try and help. Her daughter BJ was with her, fighting back tears. Add in my parents, siblings, and Ninfa, and the first few dark days turned lighter. Still, I lay there each night, rotating my ass off and wondering how I was going to get out of this mess. The only answer I came up with was: *I'm not.*

Whenever I had a visitor, I hoped the doctors or nurses wouldn't appear to lift up my sheet and check out my privates for some reason. By now, I was just a cadaver, something for them to inspect. I'm sure they were doing what they needed to do to keep me healthy, but when you're sixteen and someone constantly lifts up your blanket to check out your genitals, it's unnerving. Fortunately, they never did expose me to my friends, but I didn't know that they wouldn't.

Another constant worry was if I would mess myself while a visitor—especially Allison—stood next to me. I assumed it was hard to have a girlfriend if she saw you crap yourself.

By the third week in, my halo and thirty-five-pound weight were gone. Through a tremendous amount of work and strain, I was able to slide into a wheelchair. Sure, it took two people helping me—but it was something to build on.

My daily routine settled into a grind. I did therapy eight hours a day. First thing in the morning, I saw the respiratory therapist, Elena Ravich. I wasn't making much progress, mainly because my diaphragm was mostly paralyzed. Still, I did my best to clear out any fluid that had built up overnight in my lungs. Elena came back in the afternoon and the evening before she left for the day. She was determined to help me recover.

Next up was Sheri Jones and occupational therapy. She started me on a simple task, like trying to hold something so I could eat in the cafeteria. It was next to impossible.

After her was Christy Avalon, the physical therapist. Christy was the hardest because she worked me physically. It was her job to get me strong enough to get up and into my wheelchair. After several days, I was able to roll to the cafeteria. That meant having food again.

My first trip there, I learned that our six-man room was one of many in the rehab clinic. At lunch, I saw other men and women. Every one of us looked lost.

The nutritionist started me out with mush. The first time I ate it, I barely made it back to my bed before it all came out. The nurse assured me it was like that for everyone. Of course, Closed Casket was there to remind me of the stink. And with the gauze out, I could smell it too.

After lunch, it was more respiratory therapy, occupational therapy, and physical therapy. Classroom instruction was mixed in. They taught me about my new body and my new life. Many times, the subject was sobering.

With my ability to get in a wheelchair, I could mingle with the other guys in my room. I was still struggling, my arms and hands barely working, but I could get around without help from a nurse so long as I applied some concentration. And the chair rolled easily on the smooth, level floors. I was by no means fast, but with all the time in the world and no place to be, I managed.

My first stop was State Farmer. Thirty days from discharge, he was excited and nervous about it. "My house is being modified to allow me to stay there," he told me.

"What do you mean?" I asked

"The air conditioning is being upgraded, and the doors are being knocked down and widened. Plus, there's a ramp being built up front to get me in."

"Gosh," I said, "I never thought about all that. Who pays for that?"

"My savings account does."

"What happens if you don't have the money?"

He rolled closer and whispered. "That's another reason Closed Casket is always mad. He had an apartment. He's lost that by not paying rent. Now he has no place to go."

"What happens then?" I asked, not wanting to hear the answer.

"There are places they can send them. Nursing homes. He'll likely die there."

"Oh man," I said, thinking about my friends and family. They had set up a fund at a local bank. So far, it held $5,000. I didn't know how far that would go in fixing my home, but I hoped it was enough. I had always taken them for granted, but not anymore. Their help and the money they provided were my tickets out.

"Come on," he said. "Let's roll over to Rodeo Man."

When we arrived at his bedside, I said hi. Because he'd been admitted when I was, he could lean himself up. Still, he was worse off than me.

"Hey, Ray," he said, not overly excited to see us.

"Whoa," State Farmer said, turning to me. "We heard you set some track records. In here, you're no longer Ray. We're calling you Roadrunner. You know—beep, beep."

"I think that was before my time," I said, unhappy with the nickname. I was fixed on Joe Montana, or at least Joe Cool.

"Yeah," State Farmer said, "it may have been before your time, but it wasn't before ours. So deal with it."

We chuckled.

I gazed up at Rodeo Man. "Did you win any rodeos?"

"Damn straight! I have a closet full of belt buckles. Only two bulls ever got the best of me—Typhoon and the one that put me in here, Maniac."

"Do you just ride bulls?" I asked, staying in present tense.

"No, I do some steer wrestling. Got a punctured lung from that. I also do some bronc riding, but the bulls pay the most and get the best-looking girls."

"Are you married?" I asked.

"No. I have a girlfriend. Her name is Crystal and she's stayed with me through thick and thin—especially when I was down and not winning."

"Where is she now?" State Farmer asked.

"She lives in my travel trailer, but since I'm not there to work it, my best friend is letting her stay in a guest room. She's a professional dancer—works mostly at nights, so she comes and goes."

"I've seen her," State Farmer said. "She's a looker."

I was about to ask another question when this gorgeous blonde slid back the curtain. "Hello, men. Are we having a prayer meeting or something?"

"Crystal!" Rodeo Man said. "We were just talking about you. You know State Farmer, and this kid is Roadrunner."

Crystal smiled. "I'm sure you guys have real names, but I'll just say hello, gentlemen."

"It's time for us to go visit Rockstar," State Farmer said. "We'll give you some privacy."

We rolled down and found Rockstar snoring. Not wanting to bother him, we hovered near the double doors to the cafeteria for five minutes. That's when we heard the sobbing.

"Come on," State Farmer said. "I got a bad feeling about this."

He rolled ahead of me, my arms struggling to keep up. By the time I arrived, Rodeo Man was spilling his guts.

"Crystal left me," he blurted out between sobs. "Somehow she hooked up with my best friend."

"The calf roper?" State Farmer asked.

"Yeah, the piece of shit! He was supposed to be guarding my girl, but instead, he took her his own."

"I'm so sorry," State Farmer said. "But there are plenty of fish in the sea."

This brought on more sobs. "But I'm a rodeo star who can't rodeo no more. And when we first hooked up, Crystal told me she'd never ridden a bull like me. Now I can't be that stud in bed. I'm through!"

Hearing this drained the blood from my face. What would a girl see in me? Why would they want to spend any time with me? Could I even have children? It was tough to think about.

Yet Rodeo Man wasn't done. "And I can't change a girl's tire or be the man of the house. Hell, I can't even change a lightbulb. All a girl has to look forward to is changing my catheter and wiping my ass."

Each time he spoke, it was another slap in my face. I had thought about these things, but not too much. I kept thinking there was a magic pill around the corner that would make it all better. Apparently, there wasn't.

As I rolled away from Rodeo Man, I needed some comforting myself. I didn't want anyone to see me, but I was freaking out.

•——•

I reached the four-week mark and mostly got where I wanted. Sure, it took two staff members five minutes to help me slide from my bed into the chair. Then, if I wasn't being pushed, it took me twice as long as a normal wheelchair occupant to get anywhere. But I wasn't complaining. At least I had some freedom.

Between my physical therapist working me out and my occupational therapist teaching me basic tasks, I was seeing some progress. But it was very slow. All I could do was relate it to track. If I had to teach a kid how to run the 400, I'd show them how to get out of the blocks cleanly, how to accelerate, how to reach their top speed, and how to lean at the finish. The basics. After that, I'd teach them the hundred little things that would make them go faster. Being a quadriplegic, I felt like my track coach was holding up a shoe and telling me what it did. A month later, the coach would discuss the strings on the shoes and how to tie them. Forget the blocks and everything after that. I was so far behind, I didn't even know where the track was located. If I pondered it too much, I slipped into depression.

With my physical therapist working me ever harder, there were days I'd be so exhausted I wouldn't eat lunch. On days when I made it to the cafeteria, they had a nice selection of foods. One day, I was supposed to be working on a holding a glass of water. Alone at the table, I tried and I tried, yet I couldn't make my right hand cooperate. I glared at my thumb, the culprit. It refused to apply pressure to the glass. I tried for five minutes but couldn't make it work.

As I continued eating, I grew thirsty. Instead of using the straw, I wanted this to work. So I decided to give it another go.

Another five minutes disappeared and still no success. I looked around at the other patients. They were content to sip their lives away. But I wanted more. I just wanted to do one normal thing: drink from a glass.

I was almost finished with my lunch when I tried one final time. Two minutes of failure later, I looked away in disgust. As my anger boiled over, I backhanded the glass three tables over, watching it explode into a million pieces. Suddenly, the cafeteria fell silent.

"What's going on?" a therapist asked, running from a side room.

No one said a word. They didn't have to. I was the only one missing a glass. It didn't take a detective to figure it out.

"Ray," the therapist said, sitting down across from me, "I understand what you're going through, but things will be all right."

"No, you don't understand. I can't even grab that glass."

"Yeah, you will. You'll learn how to."

"Well, I'm not learning," I snapped.

"You will, Ray. You will."

"It's frustrating. Very, very frustrating."

He reached out his hands and touched mine. "Everything will be all right."

This pressed a button in me. "But it won't, will it? I won't be able to walk. Or put up a Christmas tree. Or assemble a toy for my kid. Do you know why? Because there won't be any kids. Because I won't even be able to make love to my wife. And oh, there won't be a wife. So stop telling me everything will be all right!"

The therapist just sat there, letting me cool down. I noticed the other men in the cafeteria staring at their food. I'd just said everything they were always thinking. With my anger, not only had I hurt myself, but I'd hurt them too.

"I'm sorry," I finally said, pushing back from the table. "I'd clean up the glass, but I can't even do that."

I rolled back to my bed, where I was greeted by my respiratory therapist. I still couldn't get the ball to the top. Every moment of my day, I was reminded how high the mountain was and how little I had climbed.

•——•

It was time for State Farmer to leave us. I had gotten to know him real well, since he was the only sane quadriplegic in here. His wife was picking him up the next morning, and I would miss him.

By now, I had gotten to know Rockstar. With him being on my left, we saw each other all the time during our rotations. But he wasn't doing so well.

First, he had developed pneumonia. He was constantly hooked up to respiratory machines. When we could talk, I learned he'd been drinking and crashed into a tree. The rescue crew had to cut him out of the car to save his life.

Recently, his girlfriend had come in and politely said she wanted to go in a different direction—preferably one that led away from the rehab clinic. His bandmates stuck by him, though. They were always visiting him, despite having replaced his lead guitar position. He understood. The show must go on.

Rockstar told me all about the music scene and playing in a band. It meant late nights, hauling heavy equipment, and drinking at closed bars with restaurant employees until sunrise. Many of his bandmates had DWIs. I didn't say anything, but it sounded like a sad life.

The day before State Farmer left, Rockstar whispered to me that he had a surprise for him. He wanted to wait until the main staff had left and the lights were out to spring it on him.

When the security guard made his last round, checking on us, I heard Rockstar slide out of his bed. "Roadrunner, come on," he whispered. "Get Rodeo Man."

It took several minutes, but we finally assembled around State Farmer's bed.

"Hey," Rockstar said, "we need you to wheel your ass outside. We have a surprise for you."

"What are you guys up to?" State Farmer asked.

"Look at it as a going away party," Rockstar said.

"Is there cake?" State Farmer asked.

"Sort of," Rockstar replied. "Come on, before the guard comes back."

We reassembled just outside the rehab, on a darkened patio used for deliveries. I looked around at the wheelchairs and counted five. Even Wal-Manager was there. That's when I noticed Closed Casket wheel up. I said nothing, surprised to see him mingling with us. I had seen him in the cafeteria but steered clear of him. Yet here he was. I wondered if this could be the start of something new.

"Okay, guys," Rockstar said, "I'm going to need your help. I have a package in my pocket but I can't get it out. Can any of you reach in and get it?"

"I'll see if I can," Wal-Manager said. "I've pulled many a package from a shoplifter."

He struggled, finally pulling out a clear plastic baggie. Inside was a fat marijuana joint and lighter. As he dropped it on Rockstar's tray, we all stared at it, saying nothing.

"Well, dudes," Rockstar said, "let's get this show on the road. I'll see if I can light it."

He got the joint to his mouth, barely, but couldn't grasp the lighter. Wal-manager was able to grasp the lighter, but couldn't operate it. No one else could do anything so they turned to me. "Roadrunner, can you flick this?" Rockstar asked.

"I don't know," I said. "I'll try." All of the consequences of getting caught raced through my mind. Now that I was in this wheelchair paralyzed, I thought a lot about consequences.

I fumbled for several minutes until Wal-Manager had to take a break. When he'd regained some strength, we tried it again. Sure enough, I got a flame and held it for three seconds before my finger slipped. But it was enough. Rockstar had the joint glowing, the smoke swirling around us.

"Here," he said, "pass this to State Farmer."

The insurance salesman looked apprehensive, but took it between his lips and inhaled. He enjoyed it. Perhaps it reminded him of his younger days.

Rodeo Man was next and needed help. I held it to his lips. As he inhaled, he too seemed like he'd found something he thought was gone.

It was clear having me hold it while the men rolled around and took hits was the best way. I thought everyone had had their turn when Closed Casket spoke up. "Hey, what about me?" His voice was that of a lost child—sincere but lonely.

"Sure," I replied, before anyone could say anything. He wheeled up close and took a long drag. Then I started all over again.

As the joint burned down, Rockstar spoke up. "Roadrunner, you haven't taken a hit. Come on. It's State Farmer's going away party. Don't let him down."

"Yeah, come on," Rodeo Man said.

"Nah, I'm good. You guys enjoy it. Besides, I may get high from your secondhand smoke." They laughed hard, mainly because they were under the influence.

Suddenly, we heard the security guard. He was making his rounds again, which would bring him back in a few minutes. I panicked.

"We're done," I said to Rockstar just as he clamped his teeth onto the joint. Lacking the strength to pull it out, I was about to be caught holding the grass.

"He's coming," Wal-Manager whispered. "Hurry!"

I figured I'd be kicked out and sent to that place to die, so I did the only thing my hands could do: I pushed the joint into Rockstar's mouth, which seemed to make him happy. Then I rolled away as fast as I could, which meant the ants could still beat me.

I heard the guard say, "What the…? Who's been out here smoking?"

Somehow, we all made it inside and got to our beds without getting caught. Maybe they didn't want to catch us. Who knows? I wasn't going to ask any questions.

I'm not a proponent of drugs, nor do I think they solve any problems. But that one night, each man had a taste of the life they'd never see again.

Chapter Six

After the business with the joint, I told the guys I'd never do that again.

"Heck," Rockstar said, chuckling, "you're Hispanic, and I think you actually turned white when that security guard came around."

He was probably telling the truth. I was extremely scared of being kicked out, especially since this clinic was located in Dallas and my family lived twenty minutes away in Irving. I could only imagine how far the next clinic was from Irving. What if they had to drive an hour and a half like Rodeo Man's girlfriend—I mean, *ex*-girlfriend? How often would they come? I didn't want to find out.

I sat in the wheelchair with time ticking by, missing my friends and classmates. They were having fun, visiting colleges—everything I'd planned to be doing. All I could do was look out the window and imagine the pool parties I was missing. While my friends were loving life, I was learning how to survive it.

At the beginning of each week, the staff gave me a schedule that told me where I had to be and when I had to be there. Early on, they convinced me I should get some tutoring. The idea was to take some classes I could get credit for so my senior year would be easier, especially with me trying to adjust.

Two hours each day, a tutor came to the clinic and taught me a subject. I had assignments and tests. One of the classes helped with reading comprehension. I read ten books that summer, increasing my reading speed tremendously. And I took enough classes so I could leave regular school two hours early each day. This would be a big help.

Sitting in my bed reading, many times during the day all the curtains would be pulled back. This gave me a clear view of the entire room. One day, I was reading a good book when I heard metal clashing.

"Watch where the hell you're going!" Closed Casket yelled.

"You watch yourself!" Wal-Manager spat back. "You ran into me."

"If I could move my arms, I'd kick your ass!"

"And if I could move *my* arms, I'd help you kill yourself. That's really what you need, because you're nothing but a pain in the ass to everybody."

"And I'd be glad to take you with me," Closed Casket said, getting in the last word.

Wal-Manager rolled past Rockstar. "If you get another joint, let's keep it away from that loser. No sense in wasting good marijuana on a weed like that."

I'd seen some minor conflicts, mostly with the therapists. It was me who'd probably caused the biggest stir when I slapped the glass across the room. But this was two patients against each other. I tried to go back to reading my book, which wasn't as good as the theater in here. I hoped it didn't escalate

•——•

The daily grind continued. Respiratory therapy to build up the lung capacity I'd never have again. Physical therapy to give me stamina to survive. And occupational therapy to give me a chance to have a life. Each day blurred into the next.

Sheri Jones, my occupational therapist, was very good. She gave me constant encouragement each time I tried and failed to brush my teeth. She showed me different techniques. As I stared at a simple toothbrush, I kept thinking how I used to grip a football like it was part of me. Now I couldn't even hold a basic tool like that. It was maddening.

Sheri willingly absorbed my anger. She had kids who went to the Irving Independent School District, so we had that in common. Even though I was exhausted by the time she came around, I worked hard to learn what she was teaching me. I wanted her approval.

It was about a month after I'd been in rehab when a nurse introduced me to noodling. Just like State Farmer had said, they wheeled me to the shower and pulled out a waterproof chair with a round hole in the seat. Then they pulled my pants off and slid me into the chair. Next thing I knew, a nurse with a rubber glove had her finger up me, causing a stench to waft to my nostrils. Another nurse hit the portable shower, and the deed was done.

It was weird, having someone standing behind me wiggling for a poop, but I had to admit not messing my pants at inopportune times was nice too. It took a week, but once my body was programmed to a particular time each day, I saw the wisdom of this concept.

Steve Hamberger, my coach/teacher from Irving High, came by all the time to see me. He'd spent a lot of time at the hospital, though I didn't know it at the time. At the rehab clinic, Coach Hamberger constantly reminded me to focus on the positives. "The brain is a powerful tool, Ray. Use it."

I listened to him and kept telling myself it was going to get better. Then I reached the cliff edge moment. It's the moment we all reach when we decide if we're going to be like Closed Casket, sitting in our corner yelling and bitching about everything until we go over the edge of the cliff and die. Or we can start climbing up that tall mountain in front of us and get busy living.

As I stared up at the poster that hung above my bed, I reached that point and made a decision: I was going to do whatever it took to get out of this place. That was when it all changed for me.

The first chance to put my new attitude to work was with IBM. He was a fifty-something who had been working on a ladder at his house and fallen. I wheeled over to see him an hour after he arrived. "What is this place?" he asked, still confused. I knew the feeling.

"It's the place where you get better," I replied. "The place where you learn how to live again."

He couldn't see my face until he rotated, but I could see my words had comforted him. "Can you stay and talk to me?" he asked.

I knew I had an assignment to do that couldn't wait. That's why I was surprised by the words that came out of my mouth. "Of course. I'll sit here and talk until you go to sleep."

The relief on his face was clear. I told him how I'd been just like him a month earlier. If I could get to this point, he could too. After his second rotation, I heard a buzzing sound, which meant he'd just gotten another hit of pain medicine. In less than thirty seconds, he was out. I quietly wheeled back to my bed and finished my assignment. I figured my time had been well spent.

●——•

A few days later, a nurse came to my bed and put a piece of paper in front of me. "We've approved you to leave the clinic this weekend. You have a four-hour pass."

"What?" I said in disbelief.

"Yes. Your parents already know about this. They'll come and pick you up Saturday morning. You won't stay long, but you'll have enough time to breathe in your home and remember what you're working for."

Her words were like a shot of adrenaline. I couldn't wait for Saturday. I worked harder and harder at all of my exercises that day since I was sufficiently motivated. No need for any poster.

Saturday morning, they wheeled me out to my parents' car. With the staff's help, they eased me into the front seat and belted me in. The smell of a car was like heaven. I absorbed every detail of the ride home, filing it away so I could replay it later back at the rehab clinic.

When we pulled up the driveway, I had tears in my eyes. I noticed they had built a ramp up the front steps, which made it easier to get me into the house. Inside, they had balloons and a "Welcome Home" sign hanging from the ceiling. I wished it could last forever.

The unique smells of your house can't be faked or replaced. I could only imagine the hardships of soldiers away from their homes for years. I had only been away for six weeks and it was deeply painful.

"How do you feel?" Mom asked.

"Like I've been dropped off in heaven."

Cameras flashed and my brothers and sister came up and hugged me. After visiting for a while, they rolled me to my bedroom. They were doing it to help me, but it didn't. All I could see were the reasons why I wouldn't be able to live in this house. The doors were too narrow. The carpet prevented the wheelchair from easily rolling over it. I couldn't fit in the bathroom. And it was too hot. I realized how much work this place would need for me to live here. There was no way my parents had that kind of money.

The ride back was quiet. *How am I going to deal with this?* I thought. *I've already put my parents through too much crap. I should've stayed at the lake.*

I made a decision that I wasn't going back home until everything was changed. If that didn't or couldn't happen, I'd have to go to the place Closed Casket was going and deal with it.

Back at the rehab that evening, I confided in Wal-Manager. By now, I knew his story. He'd been a Walmart manager and was getting ready for work one morning when he'd slipped in a soapy bathtub and broke his back on the edge of the tub. He was married, but worried how long his wife would hang in there. "No one says for better or worse and imagines *this* as the worse part," he told me.

Women and relationships were main topics among the newly paralyzed men. I told him about my trip home and this depressed both of us more. Yet I was determined to eliminate that attitude and replace it with a positive one.

The truth was it's easy to be positive until you're hit in the face with a new reality. This happened to me twice at the cafeteria. The first time was when I saw a young girl my age. She was in a ward with the women, who I rarely saw except at lunch. We both looked at each other and wondered how we'd ended up here.

The second time I freaked out was when they wheeled in a twelve-year-old boy. He'd been in a car crash and was now a quadriplegic, like me. At least I could've avoided my situation by making better choices. This kid was simply a victim of circumstances. It was tough to see him, though I didn't see him much because he had a private room.

Seeing things like that caused me to run back to my spiritual beliefs. There was no way I would've made it through this ordeal without my belief in God. That's one thing I know for sure.

I related my beliefs to IBM. He wasn't a believer, but was now willing to listen. He told me he was an executive, pulling down good bucks at a technology firm. A year ago, he and his family had been transferred down here from Philadelphia. It had taken some time to get used to Texas, but he liked it—except the Dallas Cowboys. He was a diehard Eagles fan, so we gave each other a hard time.

I saw his wife come in, but his teenaged kids never made an appearance. I heard them saying that it would be too much for them to see their father like this. They were going to wait until he could be in a wheelchair.

IBM told me he'd been taking down the Christmas lights that had been there for seven months. His wife had ragged on him, which stoke his temper. He'd stormed up the ladder and ripped them off the soffit, his momentum pushing him away from the wall. Panicked, he'd grabbed the ladder and fell backward, his back hitting a brick curb around a plant bed. Then the ladder had crashed on top of him. He knew right off it was bad.

"I asked the nurses what it would take to get out of here and they said, 'Just do whatever Ray Cerda is doing and you'll be out of here in no time.' So, what are you doing?"

"First," I told him, "I had to spend some time getting a tune-up on my attitude. Once I fixed that, I bought into the program and started seeing progress. If they said to lift my right arm up one inch, I tried for two inches. If they said to grip something five times, I went for six. Sure, I don't even make five times sometimes. But I always give them more if I can. That's the only way out of here."

"Thanks," he said. "I'm going to rely on you as much as possible."

"That's fine, but start calling me Roadrunner. That's my call sign."

"What's mine going to be?"

"It's already been decided. You're IBM."

"I guess it doesn't matter that I don't work for IBM. Right?"

"And you think I look like a Roadrunner?"

We both laughed, which turned out to be the best medicine he could take.

●—●

My birthday finally rolled around, which meant another pass to leave. One of my teammates threw a party. To get there, my parents picked me up and dropped me off. I could see a regular car would no longer be the answer for carting me around. Right now, it was a temporary solution.

They had burgers and chips and beans and all the stuff that goes along with it. They even had a nice cake. A lot of the kids there had visited me in the hospital and rehab. A few I hadn't seen since school. It was a great getting caught up, but still, I had to listen to all the fun things they were doing. I smiled and swallowed hard. I had been part of the buffalo herd—even its leader—as we had roamed the endless plains, eating the green grass under blue skies and frolicking in the clear streams. Yet now, I was crippled and the herd had left me behind to fend for myself. It was tough.

As they wheeled me back to the car, I realized my friends would get in their cars and go off to do everything on their own. I, on the other hand, would go back to the rehab clinic and have a nurse wheel me to the shower where she'd noodle a poop out. It was hard to accept.

My girlfriend came running to the car and kissed me on the cheek. "Happy birthday, Ray." I felt my eyes welling up. Thankfully, the car pulled away so I could collect myself on the drive back the rehab.

●——●

In early August, Christy Avalon, my physical therapist, wheeled me to a stationary car and stopped. "It's time for you to learn how to drive."

I blinked several times. "Am I really going to be able to drive?"

"Yep."

"And it will be legal?"

"Of course." I couldn't believe it. It was like Christmas in August.

The first lesson was learning how to transfer from the wheelchair to the car. This was tricky, because we used a sliding board. Once I mastered that, I started working with the specialized hand controls. With no legs to use, pedals were out of the question. The hand controls would take their place.

It was extremely hard to shut my mind off from sending signals to my legs. I wanted to stomp on the brake, but couldn't. It was frustrating. It took days and days to rewire my brain.

Once they had confidence I could do it, Christy switched me to a customized van and let me practice in a large parking lot. It was a nerve-wracking experience. After all, I was here because of a car accident. Yet I found it encouraging, because I was experiencing freedom. I could see that I would have some semblance of a normal life. Where I'd come up with the money for a van, I had no idea.

By now, I received weekend passes each week. Sunday night was the time everyone gathered around and I told them what I'd done. Wal-Manager, Rockstar, and Rodeo Man also had passes, so we all told stories. One of the stories had to do with my girlfriend, Allison. She'd planned an outing for us and picked me up at the rehab clinic. We went to her home to transfer me to an SUV that was packed with picnic stuff. However, when she'd used the slide board to make the transfer, I fell. Since I was too heavy for her to lift, she ran to get a neighbor's help. The neighbor was kind and it all worked out. Allison and I laughed about it, but I spent the rest of the trip wondering how I could tie up such a cute, wonderful girl like this for life. Moving me around, cleaning me up, making my meals, and noodling my poop. At that moment, I didn't want to face it. But I knew how this story needed to end. One way or another, I would make sure she had a happy ending. At least one of us deserved that.

●——●

Talk among the fellow quads focused on how we were going to live in our homes. Modifications would be extensive. My family had discovered that the window units weren't going to cut it. We needed a huge air conditioning system installed with complete duct work. The contractors were talking big money.

I knew we had raised $10,000 in donations and fundraising events. I was thankful for that. Some generous neighbors had also helped Dad put in the ramps and were adding on a room and a large bathroom. Still, we needed much more work.

My parents grabbed all the overtime they could get, but it wasn't enough. After studying the figures, they finally decided they had no choice but to drain down their retirement accounts by $20,000. I didn't know it at the time, but there were penalties for pulling money out. Man, the ramifications of leaving the lake to go to a party were wide and far-reaching.

●———●

It was late August and school was fast approaching. I knew I wouldn't be attending any time soon. The clinic had a tutor coming in to teach me the classes I should be taking. With the ones I'd knocked out so far, I would have a much lighter load.

One Sunday afternoon after another family outing, I was sitting in my chair. The rest of the guys in my room were gone—except for IBM, who was in the cafeteria visiting his family. That's when Closed Casket wheeled by. He was worse off than I was, so he struggled more to move his chair.

I looked up from a book I was reading and caught his eyes. It seemed like he wanted to talk, especially since he never had any family or visitors at the clinic. I decided to give it a try.

"I have some books over there if you want to read one."

"Nah, never been much of a reader."

Instead of rolling by, he stopped. I decided to keep talking. "So, how are you getting along?"

"Not so good. And even if I do get good enough to get out of here, the place I'm going to is a warehouse for the poor. They'll feed me until I die, which couldn't come soon enough."

"How did your accident happen?" I asked.

"A motorcycle accident. A car pulled into my lane and hit me."

"Maybe that driver's insurance will pay to help you?" I suggested.

"No, I was weaving in and out of traffic. And I was speeding. The cops said it was my fault. The other driver is suing me, even though I don't have any money. If they win and I don't pay, they'll prevent me from ever getting a driver's license. Like I need one now."

"State Farmer told me your family had been planning a funeral when the docs saved you. Don't you have family?"

"No," he said, looking down. "I was an orphan. Adopted when I was seven. But after a few months, they gave me back to the agency. Kind of like a one-year warranty. I stayed with different foster families until I bounced out of the system at eighteen and got a job in construction. I don't have any family, so no one was planning a funeral. The hospital had signed papers to have my body taken to the morgue, where I'd be dropped into a pauper's grave. But I surprised them and survived. Lucky for me, huh? I have all this to look forward to."

I rolled closer. "Look, both of us have drawn a bad hand. But we still have cards to play. And at least we did it to ourselves. What about that twelve-year-old kid we saw in the cafeteria? He was in a car crash. What did he do wrong? Nothing."

He remained silent, staring at his crippled hands.

"What's your real name?" I asked him. "I'm tired of calling you Closed Casket."

"Russell."

"Russell, let me tell you the truth. I couldn't make it through this without my faith in God. I pray all the time and my family prays for me. Do you believe in God?"

"No, because if there was a God, He wouldn't have let this happen to me."

"Well, Russell, I have good news for you. There is a God and He loves you very much. But He gives us free will to do all the crazy and stupid things we do. Yet He's always waiting for you to come home, to seek Him out, to ask for His forgiveness. Yeah, I had to work through my anger and frustration. But now I'm ready to have a life and it's glorifying His name."

"I-I've done a lot of things in my life," he stammered. "No way I could ever be forgiven."

"None of us deserve to be forgiven. It's God's grace—something He gives us for free because He loves us. All you have to do is accept Jesus Christ as your savior."

"I'll think about it," he mumbled.

"Don't think too long. It's a limited time offer, available only while we're alive."

"Okay," Russell said as he rolled away.

I thought how tough it would be, to be rejected all of your life. No wonder he didn't see any hope. Yet Jesus was rejected and wrongly killed so He could give all of us hope and save us through His blood. All I could do for Russell was hope and pray I had made a difference.

Chapter Seven

It was another Texas scorcher. Outside, it was over one hundred degrees. But inside it was sixty-two. I couldn't decide which was worse.

Rolling through the double doors, I almost ran into my mother.

"Ray!" she said, stepping back.

"Mom!" I replied, just as shocked. "I thought you weren't coming 'til later."

"I got away early. Let's go talk in the dayroom. It's a little bit warmer in there." She had a jacket on, which made her look odd coming in from one-hundred-degree heat. We found a quiet spot and she sat down.

"Where's Dad?" I asked.

"He picked up another shift. He may have to come tomorrow."

I cringed. More shifts. More work. My parents were paying the price.

"Listen, Ray. I need to tell you a few things."

I sensed it was serious. "Sure, Mom. What's up?"

"It's Debbie. She says she's not going back to school. She wants to stay here and take care of you."

That hit me hard. Debbie was about to make a huge sacrifice. "Mom, she really needs to go to college and get a degree."

"That's what I told her, but she wouldn't hear of it. Then Ninfa had something to add."

I wasn't sure I wanted to hear it. This was spiraling out of control.

"She was going back to Mexico, but she's decided to stay and take care of you. When I told Debbie about this, she said she would still stay but she'll attend Northlake—where Joel works. With Ninfa and your sister helping out, plus David, I think we can handle whatever we need to do for you."

I was speechless, almost crying. Basically, my sister was giving up her college life at Angelo State University for me. And worse, Ninfa was giving up her chance to get married and have children. She was in her late twenties and single. She had raised me from the time I was three. She was like family. It was her time to find a life. God knows she deserved it.

"Mom, I can't believe Ninfa is staying. Does she know what she'll be doing?"

"She does. She looks at you as one of her children. She can't just up and leave you in your time of need. Debbie will live with Ninfa in her old room. With me working days and your dad working nights, we'll manage somehow."

This was a lot for me to process. We talked for a while longer, but my mind was preoccupied. So many people were helping me that I couldn't imagine what life would be like without a wonderful family and caring friends.

Actually, I could.

I'd be like Russell—aka, Closed Casket.

Over the next few weeks, I received updates on the modifications at home. The extra room my dad and a neighbor were building was almost complete. A roofer was reframing the house to extend the roof over the new room, adding tiles to match our existing roof. My mother's cousin helped out with the air conditioning, upping the tonnage to match the rehab clinic's bone-chilling temperatures. I shuddered to think how Mom, Debbie, and Ninfa would handle the sixty-two degrees. They could barely stand being in the clinic longer than five minutes.

Due to some code requirement, construction was also taking place on the rear entrance to the house. There had to be two ways out of the house for me in case of a fire.

Dad came up and saw me. He explained they were widening the interior doors and removing the carpet. "It's not going to be perfect," he said, "but you'll be able to get around."

Then there was my favorite redhead, Joyce Read. Somehow, she'd talked a store out of a free queen-sized mattress—the special bed I needed. It had thick foam padding that prevented pressure sores. Once that was done, she'd talked to some guys she knew to help out with an exercise pool in the backyard. It wasn't free, but my parents weren't filing bankruptcy either. At least, not yet.

Everyone helped out. Neighbors. Teammates. School buddies. Their selfless donation of time, materials, and money was staggering. Now, when I hear the word "community," I get it.

I wanted to be onsite to encourage everyone. Instead, I had to be satisfied with hearing about their hard work from my visitors. Their efforts inspired me push myself harder, to get better faster.

When most of the work was done, especially the air conditioning, the clinic allowed me to stay overnight. As I rolled inside my home, it felt weird. I could see all the changes and work they still had left. Nothing was like what I had at rehab. *Is this the way I'm going to live the rest of my life?* I thought.

I'd come to appreciate the frigid clinic I'd once wanted to leave. They had everything I needed there, and it was at my beck and call. At home, I'd have to live with whatever we had. There wouldn't be a team of nurses to fix things and make it all better.

During this first night, my family and I realized that I'd have to come home many times and try things out to make sure it was ready for me to live in. There were too many details that weren't right.

Before this first night, nurses came to the house to train Mom, Ninfa, Debbie, and David. They called it Family Training. Even Dad took some lessons, learning how to stick a catheter in me. Ninfa had wiped me when I was a baby, but having my family members touch my private parts was another barrier I'd have to break through in readjusting to my new life.

At dinner that night, another sensitive subject came up. "You know, school is starting next week," Mom said. "Your nurse told us you weren't ready, but they might start a transition period in late September. What do you think about that?"

"I don't know. I thought coming home would be easy. But I'm seeing that I'll have to think through new places. I need to have a plan for going to the bathroom and getting around."

"That's why they're looking at taking baby steps," she said.

"Yeah, that's what they told me in the classes. I guess it didn't really hit me until now."

"I'll wheel you around if you want me to," Ninfa suggested.

"I hope that won't be necessary," I said. Actually, I prayed I wouldn't need *anyone* to push me around.

●——●

School had been in session for a few weeks when I made the trip in a clinic van. It was a warm Tuesday in September. The male nurse driving the van helped me get to the front office. Once I was there, several teachers and administrators descended upon me.

"Welcome back, Ray," the principal said. "We missed you."

"Yes," a teacher added. "How are you feeling?"

"Nervous, but ready," I replied. They all smiled.

The principal moved closer. "You'll do fine, because we're going to make this as easy as we can. We have a notetaker who will sit in each class and take notes for you. You can study those for your tests."

"Sounds great," I said. "I can't wait."

I was thirty minutes early so I had some space to calm down. Feeling the nerves, I needed the time.

It was strange. I'd roamed these halls as class president, a record-setting track star, and the new starting quarterback. Now, I was just Ray Cerda, Jr.—a quadriplegic in a metal chair. What a difference four months could make.

As I waited for the students to arrive, I stared down at a statue in my lap. The statue was made from toothpicks. It was a bull. Rodeo Man had given it to me, wishing me good luck as I'd left the clinic. I didn't ask if he'd put it together, because I was pretty sure he hadn't—especially since his hands were worse off than mine.

Rockstar had also wished me good luck. Instead of giving me a present, though, he wanted me to see if I could score some weed for him.

"No way!" I told him. "Besides, Irving High isn't like that."

"Sure, Roadrunner," he said sarcastically. "You just keep telling yourself that."

With ten minutes before Homeroom, I started the long crawl toward my assigned room. It was like being in the twilight zone, watching classmates dodge my wheelchair before realizing it was me. Many of them stopped, speechless, with mouths hanging open. Eventually, they managed my name and greeted me before dashing off with stunned looks on their faces. I even heard various comments behind my back—or, in this case, behind my wheelchair.

"I can't believe that's Ray Cerda. *And* in a wheelchair."

"I heard he died and they brought him back to life."

81

"He'll never walk again. That's for sure."

"I wonder what his life is like?"

"I wonder what his life *will be* like."

I didn't hold it against them. After all, it was a shock to me too. One thing was clear to everyone: the old Ray Cerda was gone, and he wasn't coming back.

Homeroom and the first two periods went smoothly. Then the bell rang for the next class. I rolled myself around, with several friends giving an occasional push.

"Where's the elevator?" I asked my good friend Kyle. "My next class is math. It's on the second floor."

"I don't know," he said. "I've never had to use it."

We rolled around until we learned the incredibly bad news: the school didn't have an elevator. It had been built before the code required it and the school had never been updated. The only option was to send my notetaker to class while I went to the front office to discuss the situation.

The principal was embarrassed, but determined to find a solution. "We'll have to reassign your classes to the first floor," he said sternly.

"Okay," I said. "That's why we're easing into this. I'm scheduled to come back Thursday."

"What do you do about Monday, Wednesday, and Friday classes?" the principal asked. "You'll miss that material."

"I have tutors at the clinic. Although it would be helpful to have the notetaker attend the classes I miss."

"Sure. I'll make that happen," he promised.

I was going to need all the help I could get.

"Well, how was it?" Rockstar asked as I rolled through the double doors. "Did you score me some weed?"

"I can't believe it, but one of the cutest cheerleaders offered to buy some—a quarter pound, I think. She's getting it from the truck and will be right in."

"No way!" he said, rolling through the double doors to wait on his fantasy.

"That's cruel," Rodeo Man said. "His drugged-out brain will wait there all day before figuring out she's not coming in. Of course, that's assuming he remembers why he went out there."

"We won't remind him," I said, laughing.

"Well, how was it?" he asked.

"Strange. At lunch, I rolled into the cafeteria and the entire place went silent. Every kid there stared at me. You would've thought I was a monster."

"That's scary."

"The only time I've ever seen a cafeteria completely quiet was in junior high. We were forbidden to talk in the cafeteria. If you got caught talking, they put you up against the wall. 'Hold the wall!' they'd bark, ripping our chair away from us. It was crazy, like we were being frisked. Then the principal came by with his paddle and swatted us in front of everyone in the cafeteria."

"Man, that sounds like a horror show."

"It sure made us behave," I said.

"No doubt."

I filled Rodeo Man in on the rest of the day. He soaked up every detail, especially since he had completed school long ago and had nothing to do or think about but rehab.

"How are you progressing?" I asked him.

"Okay. Not as good as you. I just don't have the enthusiasm for it."

"Come on," I urged. "Get on with your life and play the cards you've been dealt. See what you can achieve."

He frowned. "I keep telling myself that, but thinking and doing are two different things."

"Don't turn into Closed Casket," I said. "That's not you."

I continued to try and motivate him. However, it was an uphill battle. This brave man who'd ridden many a wild bull had come face-to-face with his toughest foe: quitting.

That night as I drifted off to sleep, thoughts of school came floating back. Suddenly, I landed back at the intersection of the B and E hallways. Only this time, I was the trim, fit athlete of my junior year. For one beautiful night, I could walk and run and throw a football. It was so real it was magical. Then the nurses came and woke me up.

I blinked several times, hoping the dream had been real.

It wasn't.

Now it was back to work.

●——●

The first week of October arrived and I was ready to be discharged. Living at home full time was about to happen. I could hardly believe it.

My last afternoon at the clinic, the nurses came in and told me to come to the lunchroom. As I rolled in, I spotted a small cake with candles. Rodeo Man and Rockstar were parked around the table. So was IBM. Wal-Manager had been discharged two weeks earlier and we held a party for him. That's why I'd known this was coming.

"Time to light the candles, Ray," Sheri said. Behind her stood Christy and Elena.

"We put one candle for each week—fourteen in all," Christy said.

"And you'd better be able to blow them all out," Elena, my respiratory therapist, added.

"I'll do my best."

I drew in the deepest breath I could—about fifty percent of a normal lung—and let it go. All but one went out.

"Thirteen," a voice from behind me remarked. "That's an unlucky number."

I spun my chair around and saw Closed Casket rolling in. "You going to join us?"

"Yeah," he said. "I figured if a lazy kid like you can make it out of here, I probably can too."

I noticed the staff's stares. No one said a word. They were too stunned.

"Speech!" Rockstar said. "Speech."

I cleared my throat and thought about it. I wanted my words to count. "First, I want to thank the staff. I couldn't imagine doing this without you. Sheri, you're like family to me now. I mean that." I could see tears forming in her eyes. "At first, I felt sorry for myself. Sometimes I even got angry at you folks. But you stayed with it, encouraging me each day while pushing me to do more. I don't know how the rest of my life will turn out, but I can tell you for sure I'll remember each of you."

A few people clapped.

"Now, to my comrades at arms. We've seen a lot of ups and downs. And we've seen a lot of front sides and backsides." Everyone laughed. "I'm pretty sure we'll go our separate directions, and I hope each of you will pray to God for guidance and healing. I also hope you adjust well to your family or whoever you're going to live with."

I turned to my roommates. "Rodeo Man, may your life be filled with bulls you conquer. Rockstar, may your life be filled with happy tunes and perhaps a love song. IBM, may you get back to the corporate world and master the profit monster while enjoying your family. And last but not least, Closed Casket. You could've thrown in the towel, but you didn't. Now you're going to do something with your life, something special. May you turn your hand into a straight flush and beat all of us!"

"Thanks," he said.

"I really mean it," I said. "You can do this."

"I know. And thanks to you, I'm checking out the God stuff we talked about."

"You won't be sorry Closed Ca—I mean, Russell."

"You might be right. Now make us proud by getting out there and beating that nasty coyote."

"Beep! Beep!" I said to more laughter.

"Hey," Sheri said, "can we stop the lovefest and cut the cake before the candles melt into it? I worked hard today so I could afford all these extra calories."

"Then let us eat cake," IBM declared.

It was a special time with a special group. I couldn't imagine what going off to war was like, but this felt like one to me. I was thankful to God I was going home.

Shortly after the cake was devoured, Mom and Dad arrived and thanked everyone. Then they loaded me in the car and we drove away. I wanted to look back, but I couldn't turn my head. I guess it was kind of appropriate. The rest of my life was in front of me.

Chapter Eight

Seeing the changes my family had made to the house was a stunning experience. My new bedroom was spacious and easy to maneuver around. And the workout room was a bonus. This allowed me to continue my workouts when I came home from school.

In the backyard, a brand new pool was a gift from heaven. Quadriplegics do well in pools. Water exercises are easy and excellent for strengthening the muscles that still work. However, the first time I was put into a pool was surreal, if not frightening. Without my wheelchair-turned-security-blanket to reach out and touch, I lacked confidence. I found myself floating in the middle of the pool without the ability to get out. It was very possible I could drown. But in no time, I was able to swim like a fish. Friends and relatives who came over couldn't believe I was paralyzed. I was grateful to my parents and Joyce Read for the modifications. Soon, the entire family hopped in and had fun.

At the same time I moved home, I started attending school full time. The kinks had all been worked out. I knew how to get to where I needed to be after each class. To help with going to the bathroom, I had Ninfa put on an external catheter. This allowed me to urinate into a bag strapped to my leg. The whole contraption was quiet and easy.

After each lunch, I wheeled myself into the bathroom and emptied the leg bag into the commode. Then I was able to make it until I came home, where Ninfa would remove the external catheter and stick in an internal one. The next morning, we repeated the process.

Over time, I didn't even think about the catheter. Two years later, I had improved enough to put the external catheter on by myself. That was a big accomplishment.

As I moved around campus, I appreciated even more the hard work my physical therapist had put me through. She had taught me how to jump over curbs, move up hills, and control downhill descents. I certainly had a few hiccups, but really, it's amazing what you can do in a wheelchair.

At school, I plugged back into my friendships. Kyle Jeffery was one of them. We'd been friends since elementary school. I'd even had a crush on his sister. When she broke up with me, I went to Kyle crying about it. He put a hand on my shoulder and spouted some ten-year-old advice: "At least you have her brother to hang out with. That way, you can see her every day." It took a while to repair my heart, but I got over it.

I could tell anything to Kyle. And he could trust me with his problems too. We were a great fit.

Glenn Sullivan was another good friend from elementary school. He had a swimming pool where I'd spent a lot of summer afternoons. His mother would always have snacks and drinks for us. I'd learned to swim at Glenn's pool, and needed that skill now that I was paralyzed. Between Kyle and Glenn, my childhood had been idyllic.

At the clinic, I had sat in a wheelchair while my friends ran around doing the fun things I couldn't. It was only when I was back in school that I began to hear more about all the date nights and pool parties I was missing. I would hear them talk about their girlfriends or going to movies and felt the hard sting of being left behind. They had no fault in this; it's just the way it was. I couldn't hop in the bed of their truck and go down to a nearby field to throw the football around. It had hurt hearing about some of these events in the rehab clinic. Now, the details of their adventures seemed more intense—as did the pain.

All of this brought me back to my high school sweetheart, Allison Taylor. She had everything I could possibly want. It was hard to imagine anyone better for me. While my friends were running around enjoying their senior year, I sat in a wheelchair with a lot of time to think. I had already seen how hard it was for her to handle me on several outings we'd been on. Going back over those events, I spent a lot of time thinking about her and our future together. I had also grown up a lot in that rehab clinic. This maturity gave me a different perspective. I knew without a doubt that if I truly loved Allison—which I did—I couldn't allow her to spend the good bulk of her life sticking catheters in me and wiping my butt. She deserved the best. Unfortunately, I could no longer give her that.

Late in the summer, I had started pulling away from her. We weren't spending as much time together. I could feel our boats slowly drifting apart, and didn't want to do anything to close the gap. I had carefully studied the road ahead for both of us. She'd be going away to college while I stayed at home attending a local school. She had given me her heart and I wanted to give her a full and rich life—one she absolutely deserved. I knew I'd be jealous of the man she'd eventually find, but I prayed he'd take care of her the way I would have before I was injured.

I didn't confide in anyone about this for fear they'd tell Allison what I was up to. Knowing her, she'd demand that I stop it and stay by me night and day until I capitulated. No way I was letting that happen.

By the end of the fall semester, she was seeing other guys and I was hanging out with a couple girls. We never said anything, but when Christmas arrived, I was sure my plan had worked. The day after Christmas, when I was absolutely positive I'd lost her, I began looking for a good surgeon to stitch my heart back together. At least now I could wipe my tears away with the back of my hand.

•—•

School settled into a smooth routine. My notetaker was excellent. He wrote up everything and I studied his notes for the tests. With this setup, I maintained my good grades, which was one of the few things I had control over.

Getting back and forth to school was a bit of a challenge. Dad finished work in the morning and took me to school. If he couldn't do it, Glenn Sullivan would. After school, Debbie picked me up or one of my friends took me home. Each day, someone stepped up and got me to where I needed to be.

As for Dad, he always put on a good face even though he struggled with the situation. I wasn't sure when he'd snap out of it until one day, he had an idea. "Ray, I'm going to take you to a special lady. I think she can help you."

I wasn't sure what he was talking about, but decided to go along with him. I could tell that wherever we were going, it was important to him.

We arrived at a small house—nothing fancy, certainly not a place where a skilled doctor lived. Dad wheeled me inside to a lady seated at a round table. Various vials of colored liquid rested in racks set on a white tablecloth.

"This lady can help you," Dad said again, as if he was trying to convince himself. "Just let her do her thing."

The lady nodded. "My name is Eldora. Tell me about your injury."

I explained the basics of my injury, which she seemed to know already. When I was done, she took out a beaker and poured in different vials. Then she stirred up the colored mess.

"Please remove his shirt," she commanded my dad.

He carefully took it off. I watched as she got up and came over, carrying the beaker in one hand and a small brush in the other.

"Ray," she whispered, "this is special water from Mexico. There is a well there which produces healing. I'm going to brush this water on your back and you should be able to walk in less than a week. If not, I might have to apply one more dose."

It turned out that another dose was needed. I went back for a second round, hearing that a third dose might be required. Each time, I was certain a wad of cash passed from Dad's hand to hers. Unfortunately, she wasn't the last.

Dad took me to men and women who laid hands on my spine, praying and wailing. There was a lot of Virgin Mary tears and strange rituals. We covered many miles, even driving deep into Mexico. When I wasn't around him, I heard that Dad was bent over in church praying for a miracle. More than one time, he cried out loud, "Please, God, let him walk. Take me. Sacrifice me for him!"

He suffered greatly. His stud athlete son was in a wheelchair and there was nothing he could do, no money he could spend, no extra shift he could pick up at work. I was headed to a life none of us could comprehend. Like it or not, I was on a giant rollercoaster and about to go for a long ride. How it would end up, none of us knew.

These fake doctors and spiritual healing sessions went on for almost two years before I finally pulled the plug. "Dad, that's enough. I'm not going anymore."

"But Ray, this man cured three people. They were in wheelchairs and now they can walk."

"Good for them," I said. "I hope they have wonderful lives. As for me, I'm done. I'm not letting you blow any more money on this."

"It's my money!" he yelled, pointing his finger at me. "I can do what I want with it."

I raised my hand. "God doesn't need this man to heal me. He's so powerful that He can heal me on this spot if He chooses. Pray for me, yes. But no more of these people. I'm done."

He was crushed. But I had learned at rehab that even my parents had to go through grieving. By seeing these quacks, I was delaying my dad's grieving. It was time for him to face reality. His son would be in a wheelchair until the day he died.

●━━●

When I started back at school, the football season was in full swing. With my day over at two, I found myself rolling over to the athletic building. I'd hang out with the coaches until football practice started up. Then I'd wind up at the sidelines watching my former teammates prepare for the next game. Once again, the intense pain of not being on the field hit me hard. Actually, I don't remember any hit I took on the field that was as tough as not being on the field with my buddies. Still, I focused on being positive, refusing to go backward.

One day as I sat on the sidelines, dreaming about hitting an open receiver, Coach Stalcup approached me. "What are you doing here?" he asked.

This confused me, because he'd seen me here the last few days. "Uh, watching them practice. That's all."

"You can't do that!" he said. "Not at all."

"Okay, Coach. I'll go back to the school. I have some things I can study."

I was turning the wheelchair when he grabbed the handle. "No, you don't understand. You can't just sit here and watch them practice. Not with your experience and knowledge. I need to get you involved. You're going to help me coach. I need all the help I can get."

I couldn't believe it. If I hadn't cried so much over the last four months, I would've cried right there. I wanted to thank him profusely, but a frog in my throat stopped me from speaking. All I could do was nod and plant a huge smile on my face.

Coach Stalcup was true to his word. He had me on the field assisting with drills. When we went over scout team plans, he helped me coordinate all the plays that the next team would likely run. It was an incredible learning experience, especially since I had to show my team-mates how do their job instead of doing it for them. I developed the ability to explain techniques without using my limbs. Suddenly, I felt useful, like I had a purpose—like people would miss me if I was gone.

I worked hard doing my job and coaching the boys. I'd love to tell you we went to state and won, but we didn't. A 3-7 record was all we had to show for our hard work. Oh, what could've been!

There was one incident that happened during the season. It was so incredible I can't do justice to it. Instead, I'm going to let my favorite redhead explain what happened in her own words. Take it away, Joyce Read.

Chapter Nine

Everyone, including my daughter and I, suffered anxiety when Ray was hospitalized. I left that first time after seeing Ray and thought to myself, *Maybe there's something I can do to help. Surely there is.*

I went to a local mattress store, explained the situation, and somehow talked them out of a bed. Then I called some guys I knew to help out with Ray's pool and repairs at the house. These different successes were like a little train… chug, chug, chug, gathering steam. I wondered what more I could do.

One day, I passed by Frank Parra Chevrolet and thought, *"They've got more vans than they need."* I had heard Ray needed a special van, but didn't have a clue how his family was going to afford one. I just knew Ray was going to need one to experience some independence.

At the time, I was selling Mary Kay Cosmetics, so my sales ability was not that of a novice. I was good at selling to women, but my specialty was men. I just seemed to click when selling to men in my previous job.

Without a clear plan, I got all dolled up the next day, collected my nerves from various spots around the house, and headed to Frank Parra's dealership. On the way, I stopped by my mom's house and shared my proposed sales pitch with her.

After listening to me, she folded her arms and frowned. "Joyce Ann, I've taught you better than that. You're going to go over there and make a fool of yourself. I don't want to be the first one to say I told you so, so I'm not going to say anything when you come back thoroughly humiliated."

I plopped into my dad's chair, realizing she was probably right. I felt the negativity seeping into my perfectly made-up cheeks. Then something else kicked in: my hardheaded nature. I thought, *If Frank Parra tells me no, I'll talk to folks until someone tells me yes.*

I arrived at the dealership and approached the receptionist. "May I speak to Frank Parra, please?"

"He's not here at this time, but his son, Tim, is here."

"Great," I said. "Can I talk to Tim?"

A few minutes later, they showed me into his office. "How can I help you?" he asked.

"My name is Joyce Read and I'm with Mary Kay Cosmetics. However, I'm not here to talk about Mary Kay. Let me tell you what I need."

I explained what had happened to our senior quarterback. "He's going to be in a wheelchair, and what he really needs is a van." I let that hang there a few seconds, building up his attention for the ask. "Is there any reason why you can't help me with this?" I shut my mouth and stared at him.

Tim sat there a minute, thinking. Finally, he spoke. "I won't be able to help you. But if you can come back tomorrow and talk to my father, we'll see what he has to say about it."

"Fine. What would be best for you? Ten o'clock or eleven?"

He chose ten, which was exactly when I arrived. By that time, the nerves had set in. *Oh my God,* I thought. *Here I go.*

They took me into Frank's office. Sitting at a table were Tim, his comptroller, and the sales manager. It felt like I was walking into the lion's den.

I sat down and Frank said, "Tell me what's going on."

At that moment, the words came rolling out of my mouth. Truly, I don't have a clue where some of the stuff came from. I described the accident in great detail. Not even taking a breath, I went on to tell Mr. Parra that it was well known he owned the rental car place up on Esters Road on Highway 183. "Technically speaking, you can sell this van to them and lease it back as a monthly advertising expense." His comptroller scrunched up his mouth and looked at Frank. Undeterred, I kept talking. "Sir, you know very well that seeing a boy in a wheelchair get a free van from you is huge. Why, you can't buy that kind of advertising. Is there any way, any reason, why you can't help me with this?"

He looked at me, briefly talked to the other gentlemen, and finally turned back to me. "I don't see why we can't do this."

It shocked me so bad that I forgot all my prior sales training and blurted out, "You will?"

"Yes, ma'am," he replied. "I think it's a great thing that you're trying to help this young man. Can you come back tomorrow?"

"I certainly can," I said, still stunned. "Thank you very much!"

By now, I'd recalled my sales training and got up and left before they could say no. No one was going to believe this.

Of course, by the time I reached the house, my imagination had taken over. I was picturing some fancy van with all the bells and whistles, one fully tricked out. I couldn't wait to see this masterpiece.

The next day, I showed up and was taken to this massive lot to look at acres of vans. They showed me a bronze-colored model that looked like a plumber's van, with black-walled tires and an inside that was stripped clean. It looked like something they needed to get rid of. As I stood there staring at this monstrosity, my heart sunk. It felt like someone had taken a long needle and popped my fantasy van balloon.

As we walked back to the main office, I wondered if perhaps the cheerleaders could put enough balloons on it to make it look okay. I sold Mary Kay products. Maybe I could put some special lipstick on this pig.

The lot manager wrote out a receipt. "If you could come back on Friday, we'll have it ready to go."

I climbed into my pink Cadillac and realized I was going to be thoroughly embarrassed. That van was the ugliest thing I'd ever seen.

With only my mom knowing about this, I decided to tell Ray's father. He was very excited.

At this point, my quest for a free van had taken on a life of its own. Some of the Dallas Cowboys were friends of mine, so I called every one of them. I wanted a real-life Dallas Cowboy at the football game to present the van. After much finagling, Rafael Septién, the place-kicker for the Dallas Cowboys, agreed to come to the game and be a part of the ceremonies. Even though I was scared to death to ask what he was going to charge for his appearance, he graciously volunteered his time. He said his beautiful wife would be there too. With Frank Parra and his wife coming, along with his son Tim and his wife, this was becoming quite an event.

Things were really on a roll. It finally dawned on me that I should tell the football coach. I went to the coach's office and explained everything that had happened up to that point. "You have to promise me that you will not tell Ray one thing about this, because if something falls through, it'll break his heart. And I don't want that to happen."

The coach looked up at me. "Ma'am, have you talked to the Birdville School District?"

"What?" I replied, dumbfounded.

"Have you talked to the Birdville School District?" he repeated. "We can't do anything at the game without contacting the other school."

I exhaled loudly. "Well, no, sir. I haven't."

He explained that since this was planned for halftime, permission had to be obtained. Otherwise, it couldn't happen.

"I've landed the van and a Dallas Cowboys player to show up for this poor boy. I'm going to let you handle the Birdville School District."

"Okay," he said, "I'll take care of it."

With a huge sigh of relief, we exchanged hugs. As I left, I reminded him not to breathe a word about the plan to Ray or anyone else.

Somehow, though, it got out that Rafael Septién was coming to the football game. I heard that Ray thought he was going to get a jersey from a real Dallas Cowboy. He had no idea it was way more than that.

On Friday, I drove to Frank Parra's to pick up the van. I was anxious about how this thing would look. I knew every boy wanted a nice-looking car. I hoped that at least they had turned the white walls outward.

They drove the van up the bay and had me come and check it out. It was so incredible that I almost started bawling right there on the sales floor. This wonderful man had customized the van. It had wide-wire wheels, custom pinstriping, and a hand polish that made it shine like a brand-new penny. Really, it was a miracle.

The van was driven to the football stadium and parked on the track across the field from Irving High School's bench. The cheerleaders were briefed on what was going to happen at halftime. With everything in place, my daughter and I went home to get dressed for the game and answer messages from the news media calling to confirm that plans were still on schedule.

When the game kicked off, there the Irving High Tigers sat, each player dressed in black and gold jerseys looking strong and confident. At the very end of the bench was a wheelchair with a special boy named Ray. I'd told the coach earlier in the day that the only thing I wanted to do was be the one to tell Ray that the van was his. He agreed.

The first half went on forever. I couldn't believe how long it was taking. Finally, the clock ticked down to halftime. I was on the sidelines, watching Ray. He was very excited, no doubt thinking about receiving a jersey from a Dallas Cowboys player.

Me, Rafael Septién, Frank and Tim Parra, and the three wives started walking out to the middle of the field. Right behind us was the head coach and the principal pushing Ray in his wheelchair. Ray blurted out that he was going to be the only one at Irving High School with a real Dallas Cowboys jersey. I leaned down and said, "Honey, that's fantastic. But what would you do if I told you that the brand new van pulling out on the track belongs to you?"

I'll never forget that face as long as I live. Ray looked up at me and his little ol' jaw dropped. After introductions were made to the crowd, Rafael presented the van to Ray. Neither team went to the locker room. All during the presentation, the van was driven around the track for spectators to see.

We pushed Ray to the track, right up to the van. Frank Parra opened the door and gave him a chance to finally see inside. All this time, Tim Healy from Channel 4 News had been filming the presentation. As Ray looked at his van, tears rolled down his face. With his bent right hand, Ray reached up to wipe away a tear and Tim Healy caught that special moment. Later that evening on the news, Tim Healy showed the film clip and said, "You know, Irving lost this game tonight, but somehow it just doesn't matter. This is Tim Healy with Channel 4 News."

On Saturday, the van had to go back to Frank Parra to be taken to Texas Lift Aids. Before I took it back, I went to my mother's house and said, "Mom, I've got to go to Dallas. Would you like to go with me?"

"Well, sure, I'll go," she said. She walked out onto the porch and saw this new van. Then she climbed in and we went for a ride.

I must have driven at least a hundred miles before I let her out of that van. And up until the day my mother died, she never again said to me, "Joyce, you can't do it." She also never said, "I told you so."

Frank Parra took the van to Texas Lift Aids, and they installed a hydraulic lift for Ray's wheelchair. They cut into the floor to secure his wheelchair for driving and installed everything needed for hand-controlled driving. They made it totally automated. That's when

I discovered a new challenge: I had to drive this hand-controlled vehicle over to Ray's house.

I made it there safely—barely. When I handed over the keys, I told Ray, "The only thing I want is to get the first date in this deal."

Sure enough, when he got through with his training, he drove by my house, honked the horn, and off we went.

For years after this, a joke floated around Irving. "What's the fastest thing on two feet? Frank Parra leaving out the back door when a redhead walks in the front."

I've had a lot of great accomplishments in my life, but getting Ray that van is the one I'll be thinking about when I take my last breath. And believe me, he was worth it!

Chapter Ten

"Ray, you're not paying attention!" It was Dad. "Listen, I designed this play especially for you. Just run the ball right between the guard and tackle. Okay?"

He took the snap and handed me the ball. I jetted off, darting this way and that.

"Great job!" he said, patting me on the helmet. "You're getting it. I might just pull a football player out of you yet."

I was eight years old, smiling, looking up at this giant. He was my world. I spent days and weeks and months with him, soaking up his knowledge, letting him teach me how to play football. He had already turned my older brother, Chonny, into a great player. Now he just needed me to catch on.

Over the next eight years, football became my life. I played in organized games in leagues, pickup games with neighborhood kids, and hastily arranged practices with Dad. It seemed I always had a football in my hands. Now I was seventeen and in a wheelchair. I couldn't throw a football, much less grip one. All I could do was watch.

After that fall season of coaching and watching my teammates play without me, it was over. When the players had senior night, I felt the pain all over again. At some point, I discovered the hurt built scabs. Over time, my scabs turned into scars. With a body full of ugly scars, it's hard to be hurt again. Like it or not, you toughen up.

I started the spring semester of my final high school year somewhat melancholy. I had successfully set my girlfriend free while completing my football coaching career. I hung out with a few girls, but we all knew the relationship wouldn't go anywhere.

Two of my former teammates—Randy Perkins and Jesse De La Garza—were there for me, doing their best to keep me involved and motivated. They had visited me at the rehab clinic with my other friends. And, like Kyle and Glenn, they had known me through elementary, junior high, and high school. With solid friends like these, I couldn't lose.

As track season started up, the track coach asked if I wanted to help out. That was an easy answer. After class, I rolled around the track, giving tips and pushing our athletes to perform better. It was incredible how having a purpose in life made most of my problems go away.

As the runners raced around the track, I couldn't help but compare my times with theirs. Now more than ever, I was sure I would've lowered my times in my final year and snagged a scholarship at a top university. That would've saved my parents a great deal of money. Instead, they'd have to scrimp and borrow to make it happen.

During my last months in school, there were a few frustrating moments, a few events I couldn't attend. But I redirected myself back to the present, focusing on what I could control and not what I couldn't. Somehow, through God's grace, I was making it.

As the senior prom neared, I needed a date *if* I was going to experience it. I knew a cute girl, Julie Arras, who didn't have a boyfriend. One day, I rolled up to her and said, "Hey, do you want to go to the prom with me?" Without hesitation, she said yes.

We had a good time. Early on, I saw Allison there with her boyfriend, dancing and having fun. I was truly happy for her, though I felt a twinge of pain. It takes a long time for deep wounds to heal.

At the end of May, we graduated and I had my high school diploma mounted on my bedroom wall. Now I had to focus on three months of summer. It was time to get a job.

My first ever job had been at Big Value Grocery Store. That's why I drove there to ponder a strategy, parking near the back of the lot and hoping for inspiration to hit.

Staring at the large windows and seeing everyone inside working hard brought back memories. It seemed like a lifetime ago when I'd walked into the store, a fifteen-year-old sophomore, hungry to make some spending money. I'd gone to the manager's desk and filled out an application. The assistant manager had read my paperwork, then stepped back and looked at my strong body. "Yeah, we need guys like you. Let's get you started."

Just like that, I'd had my first job. They'd paid minimum wage, which was common for young workers like me. My job was to sack the groceries and take them out for the customers who wanted help. I also mopped and waxed the floors. At the end of the night, I stocked the shelves. I worked there after school and on weekends for about a month. When summer arrived, I looked for something else.

I had a friend whose dad owned a landscaping company. Early one morning, I found him getting his crews ready for the day. "Do you need any workers?" I asked.

He looked me over. "Yeah, we need somebody who's strong and physical. I need guys who can push a mower all day, and edge too. Can you do that?"

"Yes, sir, I sure can."

At six in the morning, I jumped in a truck loaded down with lawn equipment and worked until three in the afternoon under the hot sun. Man, I was strong then. And stamina? I had that by the truckload.

That summer, I worked with five other men all week long. I learned the value of hard work and what it took to get the job done.

I also learned self-discipline, establishing good work habits. Each Friday, when the owner slapped the paycheck onto my sweaty palm, it felt like justice. Somehow, the world was right.

When summer had ended, I started my junior year—my final year as an able-bodied, muscle-ripped male. During Christmas break, I went looking for my third job, finding it at Wolfe Nursery. Once again, they gave me the up and down and hired me on the spot.

The nursery sold Christmas trees. My job was to show the customers around and help them pick out the perfect tree. Besides making minimum wage, they gave me an extra dime for every tree I sold. If I convinced them to flock it, I received a quarter. I discovered I loved incentives.

That winter, I flocked a lot of trees. I also bound them up and tied them to the customers' vehicles. If a friend bought one from me, I'd load it in my pickup truck and deliver it to them. I made enough money during those two weeks to buy some things I really wanted.

But that was then. Now I was out of high school and needed a job. I knew for sure Big Value wouldn't take me. I couldn't bag groceries or stock shelves in a wheelchair. And I certainly couldn't mow lawns or wrap up Christmas trees either. How could someone like me find a job?

I needed to spend some serious brain power thinking this through.

After an hour in that parking lot, I thought about how much I'd loved coaching the football team. Maybe I could find something like that.

It was June 1982 when I drove to the Irving Parks and Recreation Department, located inside city hall. I rolled up the second floor to the human resources office. I looked through all the jobs they had available. One of them caught my eye: assistant summer track coach. I had set the school and district on fire with my blazing speed. I knew track and felt certain I could handle the job with my recent football and track coaching experience. With a crippled hand, I filled out an application as best I could. Then I said a prayer and left. It was all I could do.

Two weeks later, I received a call to come in for an interview. Rolling into the room, I met Chris Michalski, an administrator of Parks and Recreation. I could see he was very apprehensive, probably thinking, *This guy's in a wheelchair and we're going to have him out there on a track? What if he's injured? How will he set up the hurdles?* I knew I had an uphill battle.

He reviewed the duties and assignments with me, asking questions like, "Are you going to be able to show someone how to get out of blocks?" I answered every question honestly.

Chris studied my resume, quizzing me about my past jobs. I hit him with every ounce of sales ability in my eighteen-year-old paralyzed body. "You're not looking at me as a long-term deal," I told him. "You're looking at me for three months. If you could just give me a little help, I promise you won't be sorry. All I need is a chance."

Chris rubbed his jaw several times, staring at my resume then looking back at me. For some reason, most likely God, something clicked in his mind. "Okay, Ray, we're going to hire you."

Suddenly, I had that chance.

Like past jobs, I made minimum wage. I was so grateful for the opportunity I didn't care.

The head coach, Taylor Jenkins, helped with any physical lifting I should've been doing. Coach Jenkins would eventually become a fireman, saving lives. Right now, I felt like this job was saving my life. I had a purpose.

We worked at the stadium of one of Irving's high schools—MacArthur—spending our days on the rubberized track that ringed the football field. They usually had the hurdles and blocks set out, so the physical work for Coach Jenkins was minimal. My job was to show the kids how to jump over a hurdle, how to use a starter block, how to do the handoff on relay teams, and all the techniques needed to be a better runner.

The age group of my athletes was six to eighteen. It was like a summer camp, where parents living in Irving signed up their children and paid a small fee for them to attend.

It was nice having responsibility for these kids. Plus, the parents got to know and trust me. They could see I knew about running and was helping their child. And they could see the improvements in their times.

Our training ran Monday through Friday, starting at nine in the morning and lasting until noon. On Saturdays, we attended track meets around the area. Sometimes we held the meets, which was more work for us.

Because my body no longer produced sweat, I was keenly aware working outdoors could overheat me in minutes. If that happened, I'd be dead before anyone knew it. To prevent this, I carried an umbrella everywhere. I also had plenty of cold water to drink, as well as having someone spray some cold water on me. By thinking ahead and taking a few minutes of preventative care, I never had a problem despite the intense Texas heat.

The program I worked in was under the Irving Parks and Recreation Department. They had dozens of programs going on at any one time. As I got to know more about this, I began thinking of pursuing a career in this field, especially since someone in it was willing to give me a shot.

One of the Irving administrators, Doug Kratz, gave me valuable guidance in how to do my job as well as ideas about a career in Parks and Recreation. People like him gave me hope that I could be a productive citizen and not some welfare hanger-on, dependent on the government and stuck with a minimal disability check for life. God seemed to always put the right people in my path.

When three months had flown by, my job ended. As I rolled away from the track, I thought, *Yeah, I can do this.*

It was time for college registration. I didn't know it then, but before online registration, selecting college classes was organized chaos. The way it worked was simple: dozens of tables were covered with lists. Each list had the name of the class like "Texas History" at the top. Below that were the times and professor's name. When the doors flung open, the crowds rushed to find the classes they wanted. There was some minimal organization. Engineering classes were in one section. Math in another. But while you were signing up for that easy math class/professor, others were filling in the list for the fun English class with Professor Clown. By the time you got there, the class was full.

Sometimes lines would form behind a class. While you waited in line, other desired professors or times were being swallowed up. I can assure you that Calculus taught by Professor Sledgehammer at eight a.m. Monday, Wednesday, and Friday would be the only one left if you didn't get Professor Softball's afternoon Calculus Light.

There was a definite strategy to all of this. The student who didn't have one was doomed to odd hours, strange subjects, and hard professors.

During my first registration at Northlake College, I had absolutely no idea how all this worked. That's why it seemed completely normal when they allowed me and several other disabled students into this large arena an hour before registration officially opened. The place was empty except for some administrators, who stood behind the tables making sure nothing out of line happened.

I rolled from class to class, picking out the best times and subjects, bunching my classes together so I could be home by noon. When I left there, I saw a mass of humanity waiting to get in. That was my first clue I had received an edge.

Later, I learned from my able-bodied friends what a complete chaos it had been. They had a class at eight in the morning and another at noon. Then a third at four and a lab at six. They'd be at school all day long. As a disabled person, there aren't many advantages over able-bodied folks. But registering for college is definitely one of them.

Once I started classes, I decided to look for another job. My parents had been shelling out so much money that I was determined to cut down their burden. Enter Joel Vela.

Joel was my cousin and, more importantly, he was an administrator at the college. During the first week of classes, I went in and filled out an application. A few weeks later, I interviewed with some of the counselors and told them what I wanted to do. Sure enough, I got the job—no doubt due to my connection with Joel.

The college gave me twenty hours a week. I'd go to school in the morning, finish classes, and work from one to five. My job was to process the new students, getting their transcripts ready.

Northlake was a two-year college. Most of the folks coming in were new college students or kids who had transferred from another college. They needed to get their transcripts ready to go to a four-year university. For nine months, I did all that clerical work. Once again, I felt productive.

My first year at Northlake flew by. Like high school, the college hired notetakers for me. I listened in class and reviewed their notes. I wasn't earning the stellar grades I'd made in high school, but I was also working twenty hours a week. I cut myself some slack.

One new development in our household was Jimmy Williams. He had met my sister, Debbie, and was now sleeping on the floor in David's room. My brother was in the ninth grade and didn't seem to mind.

Jimmy was a character. He'd throw me into the pool and help me get out. He quickly became part of the family, bonding especially with Dad. They'd sit out in the hot tub with a beer, contemplating life.

Jimmy was a hard worker, mixing paint in a paint factory by day and acting as a bouncer at night. He was trying to save up enough money to get his own place.

One day Jimmy told me, "Your family really sticks together. I never hear one of you throwing the other one under the bus or talking bad about them to others. Is it a Hispanic thing or just your family?"

"I don't know," I replied. "You tell me when you figure it out."

He never told me the answer.

●———●

The year passed by and it was summertime again. Sure enough, Irving hired me back for the summer track program. By now, I had the whole thing down. Working for the same folks made it easy.

I repeated my sophomore year doing clerical work for Northlake and cruising through classes. During the next summer, I went back to Irving for the track job and they informed me that Coach Jenkins had left to become a fireman. "Ray, do you want to take over the program?"

"I'd love to!" I said, bursting inside. They actually had confidence in me.

All of a sudden, I found myself running the entire program. They did away with the assistant's position—my former job—and didn't hire anyone else.

I worked hard to make practices more fun. I also scheduled more track meets, making sure everybody participated in some event. But I told them, "Just because you're fast doesn't mean you're going to run all the fast events. No. You're going to run the distance events, too."

I pushed the kids to participate in all the field events like long jump, high jump, shotput, discus, and hurdles. I wanted every kid to get a taste of track and field, then leave it up to them as to how far they took it. I'm pretty sure my new system worked, because we went from averaging fifty kids to over one hundred.

Once the summer was over, I finished the fall semester at Northlake and graduated with an associate degree in Arts and Science. Now it was time to move on to the University of Texas at Arlington (UTA).

UTA was a ten-minute-longer drive than Northlake, which was nothing living in the North Texas area. Registration at UTA was the same as Northlake—*for me*. Once again it was a piece of cake. However, I found life a little harder.

First, parking on campus was a nightmare. Normally, I wouldn't care about it because I pulled into a handicapped spot, opened the side of my van, and rolled out on my wheelchair. But at UTA, the limited parking affected me when students parked their car too close to my van. Sometimes I couldn't use the handicapped spot because some able-bodied person had crowded it, and my ramp didn't have enough room to fold outward. This meant driving around looking for another spot or worse, finding two or three spots far away and parking the van sideways.

Worse than that was when I returned to my van and discovered a car so close I couldn't squeeze in between it. I would call security. *If* they responded, they might tow the vehicle. But that was a big if, especially if the car was right on the line and not over it. If they didn't tow the car, my only recourse was to wait by the van until the student came back. That might be two to three hours or more. It was a huge inconvenience, not to mention hot.

The next aspect of UTA I had to endure was the distance between the classes. As soon as one class ended, I rolled like my life depended on it. If my class was upstairs, waiting for an elevator added to the transfer time. Every day was a challenge. Forget talking to a friend or going to the bathroom. That's when the leg bag earned its keep.

One day, I discovered things could get worse than long distances between classes and cars crowding my van. It was a Friday and I was rolling along a sidewalk when a storm popped up. Rain pelted my face from a near-horizontal angle. The once-crowded sidewalk was empty as every able-bodied student ran for cover. That left me exposed in a metal chair that was basically a lightning magnet—literally the original electric chair.

I slid my hands over the wet wheels, blinking away the raindrops and trying to make some distance. Mostly blinded, I felt my right front wheel leave the sidewalk. Knowing this was a potential disaster, I quickly corrected to the left, but the front tire caught the edge of the concrete and wouldn't come up. My back wheel slid off the pavement, shifting everything to the right. Suddenly, I hit the ground with a thud.

Disoriented, I stared at the rain bouncing off the grass. I couldn't look back, but was pretty sure my wheelchair had separated from my body, leaving me all alone. I cried out for help, but no one came.

With lightning cracking and rain stinging my cheeks, I couldn't believe I was in the middle of the UTA campus all by myself. All I could do was pray someone would come to help me. *Please!*

Chapter Eleven

The rain was relentless, and the lightning explosive. With nothing to do, I watched the raindrops splashing off the ground. As water began ponding around me, I wondered if it was possible to drown like this, right here on campus. I could already hear the news reports.

"This is Fox 4 News reporting live, here in Arlington at the University of Texas campus. Tragedy today as students mourn one of their fallen comrades. Ray Cerda, Jr. was a simple man, just trying to get to class. But a fierce morning storm blew through the area and toppled Ray and his wheelchair over, sending his paralyzed body into a ditch which quickly filled with water. Other students passing by heard his muffled cries, but no one stopped to help. A candlelight vigil is planned as administrators announced counselors would be on hand to assist grieving students, who are placing flowers and cards in the ditch where Ray took his last breath. Roll On, Ray is the new phrase they've adopted. Local vendors are already selling T-shirts on campus, and the football team will wear them during the game this weekend against Tulane. I spoke to the university president, who said the university hopes to raise enough money to erect a statue of Ray in his wheelchair as both a memorial and a warning not to roll your wheelchair off the sidewalks. The president added that his thoughts and prayers go out to the Cerda family. This is Jason Avila, reporting live from the UTA campus here in Arlington. Chet, back to you."

All this went through my mind as I saw the water building up, getting close to my face. It was probably three or four minutes before someone running to class finally stopped.

"Oh my gosh," the voice said. "Here, hold my umbrella while I get you back in your chair."

"Thanks," I said, still unable to see his face.

I heard him maneuvering the chair near me before I saw his arms under my legs. Instantly, I was lifted up and set in the chair. As I regained my bearings, I could see this student was now soaked to the bone. His T-shirt clung to his six-pack abs, showing off muscled arms and torso. It reminded me of how I looked in my teens.

"Do you want to borrow my umbrella?" he asked.

"No. I'm already soaked. You keep it. If you can just push me back onto the concrete, I'd appreciate it."

"Oh yeah. Sorry."

He jumped behind me and pushed hard, the rear wheels sinking into the soggy earth. With considerable effort, he steered me back onto the sidewalk.

"Thank you very much," I said, wiping the rain from my face. "I'm late, so I've got to get going."

"No problem," he said, holding the umbrella over both of us. "Best of luck."

I rolled on, leaving him as soaked as me.

Five minutes later, I pushed open the classroom door, glancing at the clock. I was ten minutes late.

"What's going on here?" the professor asked, glancing up from his desk.

"I fell over and had to wait for someone to come along who was willing to help me. It was quite a wait." I let that hang there for the benefit of the other students. Of course, the *drip...drip...drip* sound of water leaking all over the floor caught everyone's attention.

113

"Oh," the professor said, his expression changing from scorn to sympathy. "Get dried off. We're taking an exam and we've already started." I rolled to my desk. "Here," he said, handing me a test while keeping his distance from the dripping water.

I pulled out my pencil, preparing to start, but took a few seconds to think about what had just happened. First, I didn't blame the students for not helping me. I was pretty sure several had run past me without stopping. "You think I want to get wet helping you get to your class? I have my own class to get to," they probably mumbled. We live in a survival-of-the-fittest world. How many times do we refuse to let a car cut in line, or stop to help someone on the side of the road? Even the class registration is set up for survival of the fittest—at least for able-bodied students. Handicapped folks are people we have to put up with, walk around, or wait until they get out of the way. And they get the best parking spots available.

The second thought I had was this: The professor treated me like any other student. That was the best feeling out of the entire ordeal. He didn't see a handicapped person. He saw a late student who needed to dry off and start taking the test. Every time someone treated me as an equal, it made a big impression. I didn't forget it.

I don't remember how I did on the test. I do know that every day after that was an adventure. Rapidly rolling to class while maneuvering around hurried, inattentive students was a challenge, much like a video game with me on my last life. Being an early riser didn't help.

I had used the easy registration process to set all my classes from eight to eleven, leaving too little time to get to classes. From then on, I made it a practice to take time during the first day of class to explain how far I had to travel and why I might be late to each professor. What took an able-bodied student three minutes took me at least six. There was no way around it.

I've thought a lot about that crazy day. That storm had been a rare combination of driving rain and wind. I'd been blind *and* blown off course—events beyond my control. From then on, when I fell over, it was because I was rolling too fast. Sometimes I hit an unexpected bump and over I went. There was nothing I could do but wait for a strong male to lift me back up. No woman could do it. And a lot of guys couldn't either. Believe it or not, many times I'd lie there on my side saying, "Hey, can you give me a hand and get me back in my chair?" More than a few people hustled on by without stopping. That's life. We all have our list of things to do and not enough time to do them.

Fortunately, UTA had a good-sized group of handicapped men I could associate with and get to know. Jim Wallgren was one of them. We became close friends.

Jim had the same kind of injury as me. He'd been injured playing football in high school. He'd been a safety and had gone to make a tackle, breaking his neck. All he could do was lie there while everyone around him freaked out. They'd taken him off in an ambulance and then to the hospital, where he'd endured the same nightmare as me. It sure got my heart pounding.

Jim played in athletics at UTA, on the wheelchair sports team. In no time, I was playing too. I found my competitive juices stoked, and it gave me an excuse to stay in shape.

Jim Hayes was the coach of the team. He also coordinated the program, driving us hard in training. I got involved with the very rigorous track and field program. Coach Hayes had us lifting weights Monday, Wednesday, and Friday. On Tuesday and Thursday, we worked on the track and field events. The following week, we flipped the schedule, doing track and field on Monday, Wednesday, and Friday and changing to distance work on Tuesday and Thursday. It was rough.

We had these specialized narrow wheelchairs with wheels angled inward. They were cramped. Basically, we were shoehorned into these racing chariots. But they were much easier to maneuver and spin around than the bulky spacious rides we normally used.

During distance days, Coach Hayes was right alongside us. Being a quadriplegic himself, he pushed the required seven to ten miles just like us. I loved it. When I'd worked out before the accident, I'd craved the rigorous exercise and a good coach. His workouts gave me a taste of my past life, making me feel like I could compete at a high level.

Again, like when I coached track during the summers, I had to make sure I stayed cool. Putting cold bands around my neck and being sprayed with cold water did the trick. Being around athletes who had the same problem also helped. Coach Hayes scheduled cooling breaks, making sure none of us overheated. The program was first-class.

Our team traveled extensively all over the country, qualifying for state and national games. One national event was held in Edinboro, Pennsylvania. Unfortunately, the weather was terrible. It rained the entire time we were there. We even had to compete in the torrential rains.

UTA had an RV for us to travel in. It held all our teammates, with plenty of benches for us to sit on instead of rolling around in our chairs. The RV made traveling fun.

At an event in Tulsa, Oklahoma, our driver pulled the RV onto a steep incline, allowing the big vehicle to lean to the right side. All of us were caught off guard and fell to the floor, sliding to the right side. This shift of weight almost tipped over the RV. The driver, who was able-bodied, along with the interns, quickly got us back upright. But it very easily could've been worse.

I loved my wheelchair sports team and all the guys on it. I competed all the way until I graduated, earning a letter on my jacket just like the able-bodied athletes. They awarded the letters to us at a UTA basketball game, in front of our peers and family. That's been an accomplishment I've treasured.

During breaks in our training, Jim Wallgren and I could be found in the Dry Gulch. This was an on-campus bar in a basement—dark, with no windows. It fit the perfect image of a college bar. There were video games like *Space Invaders* and *Pac Man*. A huge screen displayed the latest MTV videos, while loud music from large speakers filled in the empty space. The rough wooden tables were perfect for a wheelchair, allowing me to slide right under them. Burgers, fries, sodas, and beer were the main fare. Jim and I ate our share there and, naturally, downed more than a few beers.

We, along with our other handicapped friends, discussed the world's problems and how the world perceived us. Folks liked Jim and me because we were honest and sincere. We told them how it was. Sometimes people don't like hearing the truth. But eventually, they appreciate it.

We learned a lot in the Dry Gulch. For example, many of the guys in wheelchairs at UTA told us they were on federal assistance. Thankfully, Jim and I had a great support network and didn't have to wait around for a government check to arrive. I never wanted to live like that. We also bonded with many able-bodied students. They treated us no different, though the rough tables hiding our wheelchairs helped.

Alcohol has the same effect on handicapped people as it does on the able-bodied. That's why leaving the Dry Gulch was often an invigorating experience. A downhill ride turned into a twisting climb. Many times, I was sure one of us would fall out of our wheelchairs. We were usually going too fast or took a turn at the wrong angle, tilting too far over. But we never fell.

When we weren't in the Dry Gulch and sober, Jim and I would tease the interns, students, and part-time workers. If it was a girl, we'd start up the conversation with a question like, "Would you ever go out with a quad in a chair?" We were being silly, but truthful at the same time. Their responses were always different.

We thought we were just having fun until one day, Jim did that routine to this female intern during one of our wheelchair sports classes. Next thing I knew, I was being hauled down a long aisle and stationed near some steps while this intern walked through these double doors with a beautiful dress on. Before I could drink another beer, they were married and had two kids. That's how crazy-fast life can be.

I saw girls at UTA, but kept my distance. None of them tried to get too close. I saw other cute girls in wheelchairs, but I couldn't care for myself—how was I going to care for them? Still, I went out with some girls and had fun talking. I was always a *safe* date.

During my two summers at UTA, I continued working at Irving, coaching track for the summer camp. Tom Henry replaced Doug Kratz as the administrator. Tom helped me grow tremendously as a coach and an employee. Sure, I was temporary, but I had my eye on working for Irving permanently. They were a great outfit.

It took me five total years, but in May 1987, I graduated from UTA with a bachelor's in General Studies with an emphasis on Business and Physical Education. Now I needed to find a good-paying, permanent job. I hoped and prayed this would be easy.

•——•

A lot had changed in my world since I'd been an eighteen-year-old high school graduate. I was twenty-two, about to be twenty-three in a few months. My sister, Debbie, had married that character Jimmy and they lived in their own place in Grand Prairie. My older brother, Chonny, was married with three kids, also living in Grand Prairie. My younger brother, David, had graduated high school and was attending North Texas University in Denton, living on campus just thirty minutes away. Yet many things had stayed the same.

I was still living in the same house, with two parents who worked their tails off. Ninfa continued waiting on me day and night, making my life much easier. And I still had that van Joyce Read had finagled from Frank Parra. Even though the house seemed quiet and empty, I surely had plenty to be thankful for.

Another part of my life that didn't change was my temporary job coaching track. I had casually looked for a job during my senior year, but nothing fit my interests or qualifications. Yet good old Irving was there, welcoming me back with open arms with that summer job. And I loved coaching track to these kids. I was good at it and felt I made a difference in their lives.

When I wasn't coaching, I was in libraries or city halls looking at job postings. This was before the Internet. Wearing out shoe leather was required—or leaving some rubber on the sidewalk was more like it.

My birthday was in July and I turned twenty-three without even drawing one job interview. Finally, I hit one. This was my big chance.

A nearby city called the house and told me the date and time. It was an entry-level position, paying very little. They needed someone to teach classes and help run the recreation center. With my five years of summer experience (now almost six), I felt confident I could land this job.

To prepare, I learned all I could about this city. I reviewed current budgets and the latest proposals to spend money on new recreation projects. I made a list of the administrators and their backgrounds, committing the names of the possible interviewers to memory. Like preparing for a football game, I studied everything I could, determined to score a touchdown.

The morning of the interview, I awoke early and dressed, leaving nothing to chance. My van was filled with gas and I had a backup plan for a friend to drive me if the van broke down. Ninfa prepared an excellent breakfast with protein and vegetables. I didn't want to be jacked up, but I certainly didn't want to get sleepy—not that my adrenaline would let me. Really, I felt like I was stepping onto the field for a game. I had everything I needed to impress these people and get them to say yes.

I drove to the location and parked, arriving an hour early. I could tell from the people coming and going that they were interviewing candidates throughout the morning. I spotted several young people leaving, just the kind of person who'd be hired for a position like this. With my long-time experience in parks and recreation, I was more than an entry-level employee. Yet I knew I needed to pay my dues first. This job would be the first rung on a tall ladder I planned to climb.

As the scheduled time approached, I rolled into the lobby and up to receptionist, identifying myself. She glanced at a list and looked back at me, her eyes wide in shock. "Uh, just wait over there. They'll come out and call you in shortly," she said as she stared back down at the list.

"Thank you," I said, knowing that it never hurt being kind to everyone.

A door opened and closed, and a young man brushed past me. I studied him closely. I was dressed better and had a nice leather portfolio stuffed with extra copies of my resume, along with notes to help me impress the socks off these people. *I have him beat for sure.*

A few minutes passed when the door opened again. "Ray Cerda," a woman announced.

"That's me," I said.

She blinked several times, changing her look of confusion into a smile. "Okay, come right in," she said, perking right up.

I wheeled into a large meeting room. At the far end was a long table with four people. They sat facing me, and the woman sat down next to them, making five. All of them gaped at me before glancing down at their notes and avoiding eye contact. It was like someone had just let the air out of the room.

Wearing a perfect smile on my face, I immediately knew I wasn't getting this job. Even if the other applicants were killed in a fertilizer plant explosion, I wouldn't get a callback.

The lead interviewer—a middle-aged man—shifted his body sideways, as if this was going to be uncomfortable. Then he used a fake happy voice—one that sounds completely overjoyed to see you—to fire off some questions. The first few were softballs. Then he threw out some that might stump me. I answered them perfectly, even throwing in some facts about their current budget. All five of them had the same expression, like an alien had just popped out of my chest. I was determined to make it extremely hard to send me that rejection letter.

As they fired off their best, I hit each one out of the park. After the first few minutes, I thought of it as a preseason game, something to hone my interviewing skills. I also liked making them uncomfortable with my well-prepared performance.

Occasionally, one of the two women asked me questions, to the great relief of the main interviewer. He was running out of bullets to shoot me down. He gladly deferred to them as they asked irrelevant questions like, "If some basketball player broke the backboard glass, would you be able to repair it?"

"Yes ma'am," I said confidently. "Just like the other applicants." Their mouths hung down. "Because like them, I'd pick up the phone and call the maintenance department to bring a ladder out along with a new backboard, if we have one in stock. Of course, I'd need to see your current inventory report before I made that call. If we didn't have one ready, I'd take a broom in one hand and wheel in the other, pushing the glass into a pile. And I'm sure one of the other players would help with the dustpan and a trashcan. Don't worry—if I could handle a hundred-plus screaming kids, I could handle that."

"Okay," the lead interviewer said. "*Excellent* interview. Thank you for coming by. We've got some more people to interview, but we'll get back to you in the next two weeks."

I drove home downcast.

"How did it go?" Ninfa asked me.

"I didn't get the job. They freaked out when they saw me in a wheelchair."

"I'm sorry, Ray," she said, patting me on the back. "Can I fix you something for lunch?"

"Nah, I'm not hungry."

I went back to coaching track, driving home each day to rifle through the mail. Two weeks went by and nothing. By the third week, my mind began playing tricks on me. *Maybe one of them is fighting for me? Could it be possible I got this job after all?*

Once it entered the fourth week, I decided to call them and see what had happened.

"Yes, ma'am? My name is Ray Cerda, Jr. I applied for a job and want to know if I got it?" I used an overly enthusiastic voice, like they'd used when they interviewed me. I wanted to make it uncomfortable to reject me.

"Okay, let me patch you through to the lead interviewer."

This was perfect. I wanted to hear what he had to say.

"Mr. Cerda, how are you doing?"

"Fine," I replied. "I wanted to see when I can start that job."

"Uh... well... did the Human Resources Department not get back with you?" He coughed several times. "You didn't get a letter?"

"No, sir. I haven't heard anything. When do I start?" I asked excitedly, already knowing the answer.

"Uh... I'm sorry. We went with somebody else. You just need to have a little bit more experience."

"Oh, I understand. How much experience for an entry-level position do you recommend?" I asked as professionally as I could.

"Uh…I would say… uh… *more*. Yes, you just need more experience."

"Okay, sir. Thank you for the opportunity. Maybe you'll see me again, interviewing for another position. Thank you for your advice."

I heard a click before I could hang up. Then I pushed back from the phone and rolled to my room, where I stared at the walls for an hour.

Is it always going to be like this? Is anyone going to take a chance on me? Was Rodeo Man right?

Chapter Twelve

One by one, my friends picked up jobs, especially those who had made it through college in four years instead of the five years I'd taken. One of them even entered the military. By the end of the summer, they were all earning nice paychecks. Yet here I was, sitting on the edge of the dance floor, hoping and praying someone would ask me to dance. The ones I'd asked had already rejected me. It was disheartening.

At the end of August, my summer track coaching position ended, along with my paycheck. I rolled up to the mirror and stared at the image: an unemployed twenty-three-year-old man in a wheelchair. The feeling of being productive sizzled inside of me like the embers of a small fire, just waiting for a chance to burst into life.

I continued driving to libraries. I was such a regular patron that the librarians often had the listings ready for me. I also scanned through local newspapers they stocked, including the *Dallas Morning News* and *Fort Worth Star-Telegram*. Many times, I picked up potential job listings in those.

After hitting all the spots for leads, I'd come home to my blessed Ninfa and find something good cooking on the stove. Then I'd study the afternoon mail to see if I'd hit on any applications. Before I went to bed, Ninfa would put on a rubber glove and noodle a poop out of me. That was my life. I was her life.

On the last day of August, I received a call telling me I'd snagged another interview—my second. This pumped me up big time. I immediately started researching everything I could about the job and the city. No one was going to out-hustle me.

A week later, I wheeled into a large room to a repeat performance of the first interview. I saw the same wide eyes and uncomfortable body language. I even took some ridiculous questions like, "If you weren't in Parks and Recreation, what else would you rather be doing?" Translation: *How about finding another career?*

Near the end of the interview, one of the men asked me an unexpected brain teaser. "How many balloons could fill this room?"

I looked around and studied the dimensions. "At least five million."

He let loose a laugh. "Did you say five *million*?"

"Yes, sir. They really don't take up much space, since you didn't specify they had to be filled with air." His smile disappeared. "I like to go for the bigger number when possible—you know, think big."

The lady to his left swallowed hard and looked down at her pad to make some pretend notes.

Once again, they said how great an interview it was. "Electric," one of them said. Yet we all knew the truth. They would reject me.

Two weeks later, this was confirmed. At least they sent a nice letter.

I went through more interviews over the next four months. There were interesting questions like: "How would you break up a fight?" My answer: "Very carefully."

"What superhero would you most like to be?" My answer: "Batman. He seems like the smartest and the richest."

"If you walked into a bar, what drink would you order?" My answer: "Water. It's free and I'm unemployed." (They all laughed at that one.)

"Do you think during your entire lifetime, it's possible for you to be awarded a Nobel Prize, and if so, what category?" My answer:

"Yes, in literature, since I plan to write a book one day about my experiences and include these dumbass questions." (Okay, I left off that last part.)

Through these interviews, I learned to translate a hidden language.

"On paper, you look really great." Translation: *In real life, you don't look so good.*

"You look good, but we're needing someone with specialized skills in this category." Translation: *We're looking for someone who can walk.*

"We're going to be interviewing other people." Translation: *We have to, since there's no way we're hiring you.*

"You'll be hearing from us in a week or two." Translation: *That's long enough for us to not feel guilty about rejecting you.*

Half the time, I received a glowing rejection letter, and the other half, I had to call to make them tell me I hadn't gotten the job. It was one depressing event after another. All this for a single entry-level position into the bottom-most rung in a parks and recreation department. I probably wouldn't have believed it was possible to get rejected so many times if I hadn't been living through it.

Several people close to me suggested I go back to school, but I didn't see any sense in that. All I'd be doing was spending more money to be a well-educated unemployed handicapped person. I needed to climb this mountain right now or plan a life of government assistance and lack of purpose.

Each day, I woke up and saw Mom and Dad working hard. Chonny had a good job. Even my sister had a job teaching. All of that should have inspired me, but instead I felt inadequate. They were all rowing the boat. I was the only one not pulling my own weight, although I did have to *push* my weight around all day long.

I was at a crossroads in my early life. It was clear that getting a job in a wheelchair was going to be tough. I just wanted to be a productive citizen in society. To pay taxes. To mean something. To be a normal person like every hardworking American out there. Yet every door was slammed in my face. What more could I do? I needed one person to believe in me and give me a chance. But was that person even out there?

•——•

In the fall of 1987, I learned of a volunteer position at a nearby Irving recreation center. It was only a couple hours a week, but it got me out of the house *and* gave me another point to add to my resume. I assisted the coach in teaching basketball and doing exercise classes for special needs folks. I loved helping out—counting for something. Knowing that there was a coach and a bunch of students somewhere on this planet who planned on me showing up gave me purpose. And purpose got me up in the morning, carrying me through my lengthy preparation. I wore a big smile on those days.

By the end of the year, I reviewed my spreadsheet and counted fourteen interviews I'd attended. There were fourteen checkmarks in the rejection column. When I landed the fifteenth, I went through the same process, researching the city and learning as much as I could. The night before the interview, I reviewed my notes and then tried to go to sleep. But it was hard. I felt restless. I knew there was some tragic number out there of interviews failed that would tell me it was time to stop this madness and give in to the dark side of life, just sitting around and moaning about my circumstances. I didn't know what the number was, but I had to be getting close. It would be an uneasy night.

With my best interview suit on, I rolled into a much smaller room with only four people. I pushed close to the table, closer than I'd ever been before. This felt more intimate, more personal. I wondered if fifteen would be the magic number.

They asked the usual questions and I had all the rehashed answers totally rehearsed by now. I had to force myself to go slow. I wanted them to think I was coming up with the answers on the fly and not after fourteen failed interviews.

Near the end, the lead woman asked me something intriguing. "What question do you wish we would ask you, but haven't?"

I leaned back and thought for a second. This was an interesting spot. I could go in several directions, from safe to risky. After fourteen failures, I decided to take a chance. "Can you do this job even though you're in a wheelchair?"

Now it was the woman's turn to lean back and think for a moment. "Okay," she replied, nodding. "And what would your answer be?"

"Yes, I can absolutely do this job in a wheelchair!" I felt as confident as I had ever felt. This might be the turning point to break this logjam.

She stared at me and grinned. "What question would you like to ask us?"

Since I was so close to victory, I decided to go for broke instead of waiting to check the mail for that fifteenth rejection letter. "Would you give me a chance to do this job even though I'm in a wheelchair?"

The woman grimaced, rubbed her chin, licked her dry lips, and hesitated for what seemed like a minute. I decided to go for double broke. "Would you be honest and tell me if you'd give me the job but for the wheelchair?"

"You want honesty?" she blurted out, leaning forward. "I'll give you honesty. The second you rolled in here, each of us knew you had no chance getting this job. We run a parks and recreation department, with an emphasis on the word *recreation*. Citizens come here to play sports, learn exercises, and generally do things that require moving around a lot. So, let's pretend we hire you and say, 'Okay, Mr. Cerda, go into the gym and get this basketball game started. Oh, what did you say? You can't pass a basketball? You can't even hold one?' Hell, you can't even shake my hand. How are you going to get anything done from a wheelchair? Huh?"

I was speechless. It took me some time, but I recovered and let loose a few choice words for her. "You know, you and all the other cities won't even give me a chance to prove you wrong. You see me coming and write me off. Right?"

"No, that's not right. We didn't see you coming, because you weren't even supposed to be coming to this interview. One of my assistants accidentally allowed your name through. You see, we talked with the other cities and they all say, 'Oh man, we had to interview this guy in a wheelchair. Don't let him into an interview. He'll tie you up in knots. His name is Ray Cerda. Just throw his resume in the trash or you'll be sorry.' So, if you want honesty, you shouldn't have even made this interview. And no, you won't be getting a rejection letter from us."

This confused me. "I won't?" My heart beat fast, thinking she may have been testing me. "So, did I get the job?"

"No, you didn't get the job," she said, breaking my heart yet again. "We won't be sending you a letter because we're telling you right now. You are rejected! There's no way we're hiring a guy in a wheelchair to work in a recreation department. It would be like hiring a blind person to work up fifty stories welding I-beams to columns. That would be plain stupid. You can go now."

Someone behind me put their hand on my shoulder. "It's time."

I didn't want to leave, because I was too shocked. I wanted to keep going, to fight this injustice.

"It's time!" the voice said, louder.

I fought with the hand, but was not able to get it off my shoulder.

"Ray, it's time to get up. You're talking in your sleep again."

I opened my eyes and saw Ninfa jostling my shoulder. "Wha… was I asleep?"

"Yes," she said softly. "Were you having nightmares again?"

"Yeah. But this one seemed so real."

"Well, shake it off. You have an interview in a few hours. I have breakfast going. Come on. You need to get up and get going so you can land that job."

It took a few extra minutes, but eventually I moved from the bed to the bathroom and took care of business. Then I drove to the place, answered the same interview questions I always did, and saw that they loved me. Two weeks later, I received a rejection letter. Fifteen straight strikeouts. But, as Zig Ziglar would say, "I'm that much closer to getting a yes!"

•———•

The cold wind pounded the library's window, tossing dead leaves around. Occasionally, a limb was lifted, stretching the tree back and forth like someone trying to stay warm. The temperature outside was freezing, which made me glad to be inside, tasting that distinctive paper and glue smell that only comes from a large supply of books.

I backed away from the large window and wheeled around the library, going through my usual ritual. Listings, newspapers, magazines, and anything else I could get my hands on. Occasionally, I'd scribble down some information about a job opening, noting the city so I could drive over to their city hall and check their posted ad. Sometimes I found slight differences that gave me an edge.

"Happy New Year, Ray," Vivian, the head librarian, said as she approached me one day. "I keep hoping I won't see you again, even though I like your company. How's it going?"

"It's going okay," I replied. "But I sure prefer the heat of summer, not the cold of winter."

"Oh, not me," she said as she took a seat across from me, brushing back her shoulder-length hair and removing her glasses. "Winter is my favorite time of the year. I can sit next to my fireplace and wiggle around in my favorite chair—well-worn, I might add. Then I'll pick up a good book and a steaming cup of cocoa and dive into both. There's no place I'd rather be."

"With or without marshmallows?" I asked.

"With, of course. Is there any other way?"

I chuckled for the first time in forever.

"You seem down," she said. "Are you feeling okay?"

I sighed. "Yeah, I'm okay. It's just that I've been to fifteen interviews and each time they see I'm in a wheelchair, the party's over. That's why I have fifteen rejection letters."

"Are you telling me they're surprised to see you in a wheelchair?"

"Yes. They don't know that until they see me."

"Hmm," Vivian said. "Have you tried changing things up?"

"Like what? A new suit?"

"No," she replied. "Perhaps if you prequalified them, you might have a different result."

"Prequalified? You mean like a loan?"

"No. More like a sales lead. You see, if I wanted to buy old homes and fix them up, I could put out advertisements that said, 'I buy homes. Any shape and size.' That would get me a bunch of calls. Yet many of those people would have new homes and owe a lot of money on them, too much for me to buy at a discount. I'd be on the phone all day long talking to leads who weren't the kind I was looking for. Do you understand what I'm saying?"

"Not really," I said. I hoped this was going somewhere, not that I had somewhere to go.

"Well, if I changed up my ad and said, 'I buy old, beat-up, ugly homes,' I'd get less calls. But each one I did get would surely be an old, distressed home—just the kind I'm looking for. My advertisement will have prequalified the lead."

"Gee, that's pretty smart," I said. "So, how do I prequalify my ad?"

Vivian giggled. "You mean your resume. You could attach a photo to it, although that would be extreme. I suggest putting a note on there that references your wheelchair."

"Wait, I get it. I could put in the hobby section that I participated in wheelchair sports."

"Exactly. That way, when you get a call, you'll know that's not a big issue. You will have *prequalified* yourself."

Excitement bubbled in my chest for the first time in weeks. "That's brilliant, Vivian. You're the best!"

"Thank you, Ray," she said, combing her fingers through her hair. "It's amazing how much knowledge is stored on these racks. If people would just see the value."

"I sure do. And here's to hoping that you never see me again."

Her face brightened. "I would rather say, 'Here's to hoping that the next time I see you, you're employed.'"

I raced home and changed up my resume. Now it was clear I was handicapped. So long as they read the resume to the very bottom hobby section, I was officially prequalified.

•——•

Vivian sure knew what she was talking about. The change she'd suggested brought dramatic results. After two full months, my interviews had dropped to zero. No more false hopes dashed. Instead, there were no hopes whatsoever. I couldn't decide which was worse.

I asked Debbie's husband, Jimmy, about it. "Hmm," he muttered, scratching his head. "To date girls and have each one dump you. Or never go on any dates at all. Which would I prefer? That's a toughie. It might require a beer and a hot tubby. You up for it?"

"Yeah," I said. "It's cold, but once I get in I'll be warm. So long as we can stay in there forever."

"You know, buddy, it's our fantasy. Let's stay in the hot tub for the rest of our lives. Do you think Ninfa will serve us unlimited beers?" I needed cheering up, and Jimmy was just the right guy to do it.

●——●

Another year came and went. So did another. One day I woke up and discovered I'd been out of school for three long years without even a whiff of a job. I wondered how many years it would be before I could land something. Then I wondered if I reached retirement age without ever having a job—just sending in resumes my entire adult life—could I still qualify for social security. I doubted it.

In late May 1990, I spotted yet another opportunity. Grand Prairie had a job opening for a full-time assistant center supervisor at the Charley Taylor Recreation Center. Other than a part-time job, this was the lowest of the low in the recreation world—an entry-level position. It didn't pay a lot, but this was what I was mostly applying for. I needed to find a way to get my paralyzed foot in the door so I could roll my wheelchair right on through.

Using some more advice from Vivian—"Ray, sometimes it's not *what* you know, but *who* you know"—I put in a call to Chris Michalski, the guy who'd given me my first break at coaching summer track. I hoped he might call Grand Prairie and tell them I could handle the job or at least give me a great recommendation if they called him. Sure enough, I landed an interview. And with my prequalified resume, I knew I was going toe to toe with the other applicants on knowledge, experience, and brains. They'd have to beat me fair and square, without using the wheelchair as a sledgehammer to bludgeon me to death.

It was two p.m. sharp when I rolled into the Charley Taylor Recreation Center in Grand Prairie. A single table and one woman seated behind it waited for me. This job was mine for the taking.

133

"Hello, Ray," the woman said, getting to her feet. "I'm Nancy Brown. Nice to meet you."

"Nice to meet you too, Ms. Brown."

"Oh, please, call me Nancy."

With the pleasantries out of the way, we got down to business.

"I see from your resume you have some experience in parks and recreation. Tell me about that."

This was the usual icebreaker. I covered everything I'd done, adding important details to my job responsibilities. As I spoke, I knew she knew I was overqualified for this job. But even though I was pre-qualified and overqualified, I was unemployed. Man, I just had to hit this out of the park, because I'd likely not see a better chance to land my first career job.

When I finished, she moved to the testing phase. "How would you set up and organize a volleyball tournament?"

I spilled out the answer, hitting on problems that might arise. Then she gave me another teaser. "We're an umpire short at the softball field and the first game is in ten minutes. How would you handle that?"

I knocked it over the fence. She kept going until she realized she couldn't stump me. After forty-five minutes, she stood up. "Ray, thanks for coming in. I'll let you know."

"Nancy," I said, "I hope I get a chance to work with you."

"Me too, Ray." She seemed genuine.

As I rolled to the van, I felt like I had crushed the interview. Of course, I always felt like that. Now it was time to wait.

Exactly seven days later, I received a call. "Ray, this is Nancy Brown." She sounded happy, which caused my heart to nearly burst.

"Hi, Nancy," I replied. "Thanks for calling."

"I would like you to interview with my bosses. They have some questions for you."

"Of course," I said, barely containing my excitement. "What time?"

She gave me the details and I could barely hang up before screaming for joy. I had made it to the second level of what felt like a really hard video game. Then I wondered how many levels there were for an entry-level position.

The next day, I met with Phyllis Teakel. She ran me through a battery of questions before passing me up to her boss, Ron Neely. He did the same thing, ripping me from side to side and going through different scenarios. After an hour or more of these two interviews, Phyllis and Nancy joined Ron in his office as they asked me to roll outside so they could talk about it.

I know the veins in my neck had to be throbbing, because my pulse rate was off the charts. This was the moment. I was so close I could taste it. While I sat in the outer room next to the secretary, I lowered my head and prayed. "Dear God, please let this be the one. Please just give me a chance to show them what I can do. I'm not asking for money or a nice car. I just want a job. Just one job. It's been three long years. Please let me be productive and give me a purpose in life. Please, God, hear my prayer."

Thirty minutes later, I rolled up the ramp into my house, spotting Ninfa in the kitchen. She turned to ask me how it'd gone and I ignored her, instead rolling into my bedroom and slamming the door behind me. I didn't want her to see me like this.

I stared at my face in the mirror, the tears streaking down my cheeks. I started choking up, letting my emotions take over. Now I was crying out loud.

I clasped my hands and prayed again. "Dear God, thank you for this opportunity. I promise I won't let you down. I know you've been testing me, and I pray I honored you through all this. I just can't thank you enough."

I wiped the tears from my face and raised my arms as high as I could. Then I looked back in the mirror at a face—a new face, the one of a winner. I felt like I had just won the Super Bowl. In a way, from dying in front of an eighteen-wheeler screeching to a halt to becoming the recipient of an entry-level full-time job, I had.

Amen!

Chapter Thirteen

Before I was officially hired, Grand Prairie made me take a drug test. They gave me the address of the lab and I rolled into the lobby, telling them why I was there. A male drug tester handed me a cup and followed me into the bathroom. "How do you want to do this?" I asked him.

"What do you mean?" he replied.

"I'm a quadriplegic. I have a catheter that feeds into a leg bag."

"You can't go in a cup?"

"Dude, I'm a quad whose been strawed. You'll have to hold this tube to the cup and stand here for a while. You know, wait for whenever it decides to dribble out. Or you can take some freshly squeezed urine from the bag. It's your choice."

He scratched his head with a gloved hand before vigorously rubbing his nose. "I guess we can pour some in from the bag. You don't look like a druggie."

I let out a burst of laughter. "It's hard to do drugs when you can't even wipe yourself."

"For sure," he said, glancing sideways at me to make sure I wasn't lying.

I told him what to do and supervised him as he poured the urine into the cup. As the liquid raced to the top, I could see he was pouring way too fast. Thankfully, he stopped in time, letting the surface tension keep it from spilling over. Ever so carefully, he took the lid from his other hand and tightened it on the container. This was a mistake. It was too full. Needless to say, he made a mess of everything. It was a good thing he wore gloves.

After he returned my leg bag to its upright position, he followed me outside, studying my van. It was only when I was on the road that I realized why. He'd probably wondered if I had concocted the whole quadriplegic story. Maybe my leg bag was filled with a friend's urine? It certainly would've been a creative idea for some desperate druggie.

Two days later, Nancy called and said my drug test was clean. She wanted me to start the next day—a Wednesday.

"I'll be there!" I assured her, reliving the euphoria of being officially employed full time.

I told my family I had passed the drug test and like the urine, congratulations came pouring in. My friends Kyle, Randy, and Jesse, were ecstatic. I think they were as thankful as I was. Well, almost. After three long years, my enthusiasm was off the charts.

The next morning, I arrived an hour early to make a good impression. Nancy seemed genuinely pleased to have me there. With her calm demeanor and command of the rec center, I could tell right off she would be a great boss.

First, we went over my work schedule. The Charley Taylor Recreation Center was open six days a week. Nancy wanted me working when she wasn't there. Our schedules would overlap during the middle of each day. This meant I'd work Monday through Thursday one p.m. to closing time at ten p.m. On Friday, I had the nine-to-six shift, which again was closing time. We had two part-timers who covered the nine-to-two shift on Saturdays. If they needed off, I'd have to work Saturdays. I hoped that wouldn't be too much.

Once I had the schedule down, Nancy took me on a tour of the property and explained my duties and responsibilities. I'd be helping her with the planning of all recreation activities. It was my job to organize any special events, which included the two festivals we held each year for the neighborhood. We also put on tournaments at our baseball and softball fields behind the facility. I'd have to supervise those. Basically, I'd be Nancy's righthand man, making sure orders were carried out and dousing any fires that popped up.

After completing the tour, I could see this job fit my skillset. I'd already handled most of these tasks coaching high school and summer track, and then teaching classes in my volunteer job. Just like in the interview, I was confident I could successfully do the job.

The first few days breezed by. I spent a lot of time with Nancy when our schedules overlapped. During one of our casual discussions, I learned that Grand Prairie had received dozens of resumes. She'd interviewed twelve people, including me. "Clearly," she said, "you were the most qualified." I'd felt that in the interviews.

I gathered from more conversations that being in a wheelchair had necessitated the extra interviews with her superiors. In 1990, buildings weren't required to be handicapped accessible. They would have to make changes to accommodate me. And they did. I noticed the maintenance department had widened a few door openings and changed some doorknobs to levers. They even installed automatic door openers in front of the building. That was a big commitment. I thought I might feel bad they had to spend the money to do all that. But then I reminded myself that these changes opened up the rec center for so many other folks. That had to be a good thing.

Nancy would often eat lunch at the rec center with the field maintenance team. I learned to come early and sit around with them. After eating, they'd play ping-pong, tell jokes, and generally have a good time. This helped me bond with more people, establishing myself as one of the gang.

If there was a surprise about this job, it had to do with the low-income area surrounding the rec center. Each day, as soon as two nearby schools ended, a wave of kids washed into our center, looking for something to do. Without a mom or dad concerned about them, we became their surrogate parents.

Many of the kids were under twelve. Some of them studied while others played games. I soon discovered that many of these children stayed at the rec center until we closed at ten. During the six-plus hours we had them, they grew hungry. Most of them had one meal a day—an early breakfast at school or a free lunch. Nancy was ahead of all this and had bread and peanut butter on hand so we could make them sandwiches to eat. It was the least we could do.

I got to know these children. They were sweet kids, hungry for some attention from a stable, caring adult. With many of them having one parent dead or in jail and the other strung out on drugs and alcohol, we were their best shot at having someone who cared. We'd help them with their homework. Offer them advice. Discuss their problems. We even brought in some rabbits so they could learn responsibility in taking care of an animal—to see how it works, to be invested in something. Yet each night, I watched them grudgingly leave the rec center and head off in the direction of whatever new nightmare awaited, hoping to survive until the sun came up. Seeing these kids without parents made me once again thankful for my family support. Man, let me just say this: Family is everything! And so are close friends. No matter what your situation, you are truly blessed if you have those. I know I was.

●——●

My first month on the job flew by. Before I knew it, we were into the summer with longer days and hotter temperatures—my favorite time of year.

As a new hire, I pushed myself to go above and beyond Nancy's expectations. I consistently arrived at work early and always left late. I was determined to lead by example.

When the first report came out, I could tell from the numbers that my presence had made an impact on the community. Our after-school program had increased due to a wider variety of events we put on. The evening basketball and volleyball leagues were off to a great start. And we'd put in a solid schedule of activities for our teens and senior citizens. When a person walked into the center, Nancy and I wanted them to feel like they belonged here, to have a sense that things were going on at this place. With my first month in the books and a good report in hand, I felt great about my new career.

The rest of the summer had almost disappeared when one day in August, I remembered my family had a trip planned to South Texas. My paternal grandmother lived in Mission, Texas, just a few miles from the border, and we wanted to see her. Nancy was wonderful and let me have that week off. Mom and Dad rented an RV and everyone piled in except Chonny, who stayed home and worked. Then we took off on the long drive down there.

Debbie's husband, Jimmy, was fascinated with life near the border. He sat at the table as Abuela (*grandmother* in Spanish) held court. She was a true character, the matriarch of the family. Actually, she was the last living grandparent I had. In her eighties, she told Jimmy the story of how she'd made it to Texas.

"I was a little girl, living with my parents in Mexico, when Pancho Villa brought his army around. It was widely known that he ordered his men to round up all the women from a particular town and bring them to his army so they could rape them. The stories were terrible.

"When he appeared in our town, Dad hid me and my seven sisters under the house, praying we wouldn't be found. We weren't. As soon as Pancho Villa left, Dad put all of us in a rickety wagon and took us across the border, settling here in Mission."

She told this story with bright eyes while sitting at a table rolling cigarettes, her gnarled hands occasionally gesturing. To provide emphasis, she'd stomp on the wooden floor, which was new—"Only ten or fifteen years old," she said proudly. Before that, she'd had nothing but dirt floors in the soon-to-crumble shack she'd lived in her entire adult life.

Outside, Jimmy came up to me. "Boy, your grandmother is very personable. I can see where your father got some of his charisma from." He was probably right. Dad could sure light up a room with his personality.

After visiting with our relatives, we went to nearby South Padre Island, where Jimmy asked if I wanted to go parasailing.

"Sure!" I replied. Of course, we'd already consumed one or two beers on the beach.

The company running this operation had a slick setup. First, the salesmen on the beach collected our money and put us in a boat. This took some work as the men carefully lifted me out of the chair and strapped a life vest on me. Jimmy and I waited until they had six paying customers loaded on the boat. Then we took off, linking up with another boat that had six passengers who had just finished parasailing. We transferred into the bigger boat and traveled farther offshore.

As the waves rocked our boat, the two beers sloshed around in my stomach, making me seasick. "Splash some water on me," I said to Jimmy.

He did. That took my mind off the side to side rocking. Eventually, they moved Jimmy and me to the back of the boat and hooked us up to the parasail. Once everything was good, the boat sped up. This caused our parasail to climb higher, wiping away my seasickness. It was exhilarating. For once I was free of my wheelchair, no different than Jimmy or anyone else. The experience stayed with me long after we made it back to shore. Anytime I had a down day or setback, I'd remember the freedom of being in the air and somehow, I felt better.

I arrived back in Irving a little more tanned and a lot redder. But there sure was a large smile on my face.

When I showed up to work, Nancy called me into her office for a talk. "Well, Ray, summer is almost over and we need to hire another part-timer. You're going to help me sort through the applicants and decide who we'll interview."

"No problem," I said. "With my vacation out of the way, I'm ready to work. Give me a stack and I'll start looking through them."

Being on the other end of the interview process was humbling. I slowly studied each resume, taking care to read everything on them, knowing someone was counting on me to make the right decision.

After a lot of hard work, Nancy and I agreed that one applicant stood head and shoulders above the rest: Joe Moses. He attended college and had worked during the previous summer at the Truman Rec Center in Grand Prairie. Much like my summer track coaching job, he had been a seasonal worker. It was during this past summer that I got to know Joe, especially when we took field trips. Our two rec centers took kids to special places like Six Flags Over Texas, the Fort Worth Zoo, and the Dallas Museum. He was easy to talk to and had great references. We offered him the job and he accepted. We hoped he'd be a good employee.

Joe started at our rec center in the fall, working the six-to-ten shift with me. He was an African American from New York, so all three of us had different backgrounds and opinions. With me being Hispanic and Nancy a Caucasian, if I'd been writing a screenplay in the seventies, I would've had a hit movie called *Momma, Wheels, and Big City*. The only difference from a seventies movie was that the woman ran everything. In fact, if someone was looking for the definition of diversity, we three were it. Even the handicapped part was covered. We laughed when we thought about it.

Joe's job was to set up the activities in the evenings and run the front desk. He was also skilled enough to handle duties I couldn't get to because I was busy dealing with something else. Within the first month, we could tell he was a keeper.

At this point, I had no idea where my career would end up, but I could see the blessing of working nights. This was when most of our clients came to the rec center. I got to meet them and understand why they came. They provided me with dozens of answers.

Some came for the baseball and softball fields surrounding the center. The little kids played tee-ball during the summer and had a blast. Inside, we had a lot of clients come for the fitness center. We also held jazzercise, ballet folkloric, and aerobics classes. And leagues? We had plenty, like volleyball and basketball. We even had preschool and after-school programs.

Most of our participants lived in Grand Prairie, Arlington, and Irving. They had to pay a membership fee. Once they received their membership card, they could come in and sign up for the paid classes, or simply enjoy all the free activities we offered. It was a good deal.

At night, when it was time to close, one of our recreation specialists totaled up the money we'd received and compiled attendance reports. The next morning, Nancy would make the deposit at the bank. With Nancy in charge, we had a smooth system laid out for managing the rec center kingdom. It was exciting to be part of a winning team.

Another great aspect of our team was the after-hours get-togethers. Recreation people are by nature very sociable. We have to be. That's the job. By the end of 1990, I had plenty of parks and recreation friends to go with my longtime buddies. My social calendar was filled.

Nancy's husband, Buddy, often joined the recreation crew for happy hour and dinner on Fridays since we closed at six. I talked sports with Buddy, becoming good friends with him. When Joe could join us, we had loads of fun.

New Year's Eve arrived, and I was so happy. I had finally landed that full-time job. My boss was pleased with my performance. I loved the job. I now had great friends in Grand Prairie. I was truly blessed.

For my New Year's resolution, I wanted to take on more responsibility from Nancy, make it easier for her to run the rec center. I hoped that by putting in five to ten years under her, maybe one day I could have my own center.

A guy could dream, couldn't he?

●——●

It was May 1991, and the anniversary of my first year at Grand Prairie was two days away. I could hardly believe it. Time had flown by.

The Charley Taylor Recreation Center was running smoothly. Joe, Nancy, and I all got along. The future of the center looked promising.

It was a bright Monday afternoon in May when Nancy called me into her office. I assumed this was going to be my review. I licked my lips in anticipation of straight As. At least, that was how I saw it. But then she dropped a bomb on me.

"Ray, I have something to tell you."

"Okay," I said. "What is it?"

"I'm pregnant. I'm starting my family, so my last day is October thirty-first."

"What?" was all I could manage.

"Pregnant. You know, little babies? I'm thirty. It's my time."

"Wow! I didn't expect that news."

"We're going to keep working this center like we are. I want to make sure I leave this place in great shape. Okay?"

"Yes, ma'am," I said. "I'll do my part."

That evening, after Nancy had gone, Joe and I huddled to discuss this surprising turn of events.

"Do you think they'll give you a shot at her job?" Joe asked.

145

"I sure hope so," I replied. "I'm certain I could handle it."

"I think you could too. I hope you get it."

"We'll have to wait and see what happens."

That's all I could do.

N ancy's departure date finally came. On her last day, we threw a nice party for her. During a break in the action, she pulled me into her office for a talk.

"Listen, Ray, I don't know what they're going to do about replacing me, but you're in charge until they make a permanent hire. I want you to know that I recommended you as my replacement in the strongest of terms."

"I can't thank you enough, Nancy. Really, you gave me the shot I needed. I hope I haven't let you down."

"Down?! No way. I put in your file that you're always on and ready. You're a great manager. And you're fun to work with. If you say you're going to do something, you do it one hundred ten percent. The way you handle angry people is amazing. They leave feeling good, that everything's positive. I wrote in your file that everybody loves Ray Cerda. I hope you get the job."

We hugged and I started to roll after her.

"Wait!" she said. "Where are you going?"

"To see you out," I said, somewhat confused.

"No. This is your office now. You're in charge. You've got work to do. I'll see myself out." With that, she closed the door and left for good.

I sat there pondering my life. God had once again been good to me. All I'd had to do was show a little patience. Now I had the job I always wanted—to run my own rec center—even if it was only temporarily.

Then I got mad at myself. I had failed to tell Nancy the impact she'd had on my life. When no one would interview me or give me a chance, she'd believed in me. She'd gone to bat for me. I wanted to get down on my knees and thank her, but of course I couldn't. I'd have to be satisfied with some words in a book one day.

Thank you so much, Nancy Brown!

I hoped my career would make her proud.

Chapter Fourteen

I couldn't believe how fast my life had changed. Three years without a full-time position, then out of nowhere, I had an entry-level job. One year after that, I was the boss. It was hard to believe.

I was excited, but couldn't get carried away. I had to stay focused and perform a solid job. I also had to prepare for the coming interview.

Nancy Brown had done an excellent job putting the rec center into a high-performing status. She was a parks and recreation major who had paid her dues. I, on the other hand, had majored in general studies and was still paying my dues one year into the job. To say I was an underdog was a definite understatement. But I had two things on my side: Nancy's great endorsement, and God. The more I thought about it, the more I liked my chances.

I devised some goals and wrote them down. One of them was ensuring the center did not fall below any of the levels Nancy had achieved. Another was searching for areas I could improve and make a difference—raise the performance a bit. The final goal was absorbing as much knowledge as I could while being the "CEO" of the Charley Taylor Recreation Center. If I didn't land the permanent position, at least I'd have that knowledge I could take with me during my next three-year job search. When I carefully studied my goals, I realized I had a lot to accomplish in a very short time.

One of the first stops I made was the trophy case at the front of the rec center. It was filled with Charley Taylor's trophies. During the summer, Joe and I had been staring at them when against all odds Charley Taylor had walked in. Joe and I shook his hand and talked to him for a few minutes. His story was a good one.

Raised in Grand Prairie, his black skin meant he attended a segregated school. His mother, Myrtle, was a hard worker, raising her seven children with another man—James Stevenson, Charley's stepfather. Charley discovered sports early, becoming a complete stud in every sport including track and football. Hearing this, I identified with him.

His incredible athletic ability allowed him to attend Arizona State University, being selected as an All-American in football two years in a row. Then, having come from a part of the country that worships the Dallas Cowboys, Charley Taylor was drafted by the hated rivals Washington Redskins. It was an ironic twist that a boy who'd been unable to attend a white high school in Texas was allowed to play in the nation's capital.

Charley played hard for the Redskins, making the Pro Bowl eight times and the Super Bowl once. After he retired, he received the call he'd been waiting for. This tough kid from Grand Prairie had made it to the top. Charley Taylor would be forever enshrined in the Pro Football Hall of Fame in Canton, Ohio.

As he told me about his early life, I couldn't help but wonder how far I would've gone. A large university? A pro football league? The odds had been against me, even without the accident. But who knows what I could've been? I wondered if I had NFL potential in my genes.

———•———

Two months earlier, as the end of the summer neared, Joe Moses quit the rec center and went back home to New York. Since we were short-staffed now that Nancy was gone, upper management took Karen Fisher from city hall and made her my temporary assistant.

Like Nancy, she had the education to handle the position, even though she'd been doing administrative work in an office.

Karen was my first subordinate as a manager. Sure, I'd supervised volunteers and part-time folks. But now, I was the boss. I reminded myself to heed my college professor's words: "Be engaged in your employees at every level. Engage them for the best results."

To carry out that advice, I sat down with Karen and went over our responsibilities with her. I wanted her to understand what I needed to get done so she would know how to help me. Together, we had to manage a 12,000-square-foot recreation center while supervising fifteen full-time and part-time seasonal and contract workers. This included training them to do their specific jobs. We also had to create and implement all the recreational programs. It was a lot of work. Then I turned the page.

"We're halfway done," I told Karen. "We're also responsible for the park grounds. This includes the volleyball courts, outdoor basketball courts, pavilions, and marquee signs. And this next one is right up your alley." I pointed to the bottom line. "We have to compile monthly, quarterly, and yearly reports. At the end of this year—which is in a few months—we must prepare and submit the center's annual operating budget of $250,000. It's a ton of work. Are you ready?"

"You bet," Karen said enthusiastically. "I'm ready for a challenge."

I made of list of tasks Karen could immediately get busy on. For the remainder of 1991, we pushed hard, trying to move the needle higher.

———•———

New Year's Eve arrived, and it was time to welcome in the new year. Yet I still had not been called in for an interview. I wondered what this could mean. Did they have someone else in mind?

While I waited and waited, I had another chance to hang in the air. A buddy of mine owned a two-seater Cessna Cardinal. One of my secret ambitions was to be a fighter pilot. When he asked if I wanted to fly with him, I couldn't say yes fast enough.

Two strong men transferred me into the Cessna and away we went. An hour into the flight, he asked me to take over the controls. With some instruction, I was actually flying a plane. I felt as if I had flown before. Like parasailing with Jimmy, it was an awesome feeling—an experience I'll never forget.

•———•

In January of 1992, I finally had my interview. Ron Neely, the superintendent of recreation, went over my seventeen months under Nancy and the two-plus months as Nancy's replacement. He didn't give me any indication of how I did or how I stacked up against the competition. All I could do was thank him for the opportunity and go back to my job.

Now, the waiting began.

In parks and recreation jobs, salary compensation is not the best. It can't compete with the business world. But there is one perk that makes it easier: a pension. The more years you put in, the more money you receive upon retirement. And the whole thing is administered through the Texas Municipal Retirement System, so it's going to be there when you're finished.

I had no idea how long I'd last in this industry or if I'd achieve enough years to qualify for a pension. But I couldn't imagine doing anything else for a living. And given the uphill climb just to get hired, I was committed to the path I'd started on.

Each day, Karen and I showed up and kept the rec center humming. I worked hard to ensure no emergencies or disasters popped up on Ron Neely's radar. I had told him in the interview that I wanted him to sleep well each night, knowing the Charley Taylor Recreation Center was running smoothly. I had to back up that promise.

Near the end of February, I still hadn't heard anything. On one hand, it was frustrating. I figured if I was the right guy, I'd have the job already. Yet on the other hand, I was the boss. Each day that ticked by, I had not been replaced. If I'd been doing a terrible job, they would've gotten rid of me. That hadn't happened. If I was still the boss after one year, I wondered if I would get the position through default.

Just when I'd put it out of mind, I received a call from Ron. "Ray," he said solemnly, "we looked at the all of the applicants for the permanent position of rec center supervisor and have selected a candidate."

"Okay," was all I could manage. This was probably the let-down call.

"We picked someone we feel can handle the job. And that person is *you*."

I almost had a heart attack. "Thank you, sir!" I gasped. "You won't regret it."

"I know I won't."

I hung up the phone and took in my office. Suddenly, I was the new Charley Taylor Recreation Center supervisor—*permanently*. I couldn't believe it. Once again, it was time to celebrate with friends and family!

•——•

The end of May arrived, meaning ninety days of summer camps were about to begin. I was rolling out of my office when the phone rang.

"Ray, it's me—Joe Moses," the voice on the other end said.

"Hey, Joe," I replied. "How's New York treating you?"

"I'm not in New York. I'm back here in town. And I hear you're the big shot of Charley Taylor now. I was wondering if I could snag a summer camp counselor position."

"Of course," I said. "Come on in and we'll get you signed up."

This was great news. Joe was a top worker and someone I could trust. Plus, I loved hanging out with him. He even came over to my house for meals. That's how close we were.

A few days after Joe started, my brother Chonny was over visiting with his son, Michael. Things weren't good in Chonny's life. He and his wife were going through a divorce. He was scheduled to sign the papers in a few days, something that weighed heavily on his mind.

It was hot outside when he went for a run in the neighborhood. Chonny loved running, as he'd been a track star too. Michael wanted to be with his father but couldn't keep up. He rode a bicycle instead, following Chonny on the long route.

One block from the house, Chonny, dripping with sweat, stopped to recover. "Go put up your bike and get the car keys," he told Michael. "I want to drive the route and see how far I ran."

Michael rode to our house and went to the backyard, putting away his bike. I was watching TV when my younger brother, David, went out to the porch to see how his brother had done. David had just reached the railing when he spotted Chonny sweating and breathing heavily. Suddenly, Chonny leaned forward before listing to his right, collapsing on the pavement in a heap.

"Something's wrong with Chonny!" David yelled, leaping from the porch and running to our brother. I rolled outside in time to see David trying to revive Chonny. From where I sat, it looked bad.

With Mom coming behind me, I rolled down the ramp and had just reached my brothers when a car stopped and a lady rushed out. "I'm a nurse," she said and immediately began working on him. Mom knelt next to her, rubbing Chonny's arm.

In no time, the ambulance arrived. The paramedics worked on starting Chonny's heart while I freaked out, unable to do anything from my wheelchair. For the first time since my accident, I knew how my parents had felt when they'd stood helpless over me.

Ten minutes before all this, Debbie had left our house to go back to her home in Grand Prairie. We called Jimmy, and he and Debbie came back in time to see them loading Chonny into the ambulance.

As the ambulance doors closed, Joyce Read arrived. She had heard what was happening and came over to hold me. All I could say to her was, "I couldn't help him. I just couldn't help him." It was one of the toughest moments of my life.

I don't know if it's possible to die of a broken heart, but I do know Chonny had one. He was thirty-three years old when the hospital pronounced him dead. All of us were devastated, including his son, Michael, and two daughters, Elizabeth and Nikki.

My brother's funeral was enormous—standing room only. The line of cars was one of the longest I've ever seen. It was a testament to Chonny, who was truly loved by family, friends, and the community. Not a day has gone by that we don't miss him.

●———●

A week after the funeral, I rolled back to work with a heavy heart. I was grateful to have Karen and my good friend Joe to talk to. After I had received the permanent rec center supervisor position, Karen was made the permanent assistant recreation supervisor. She'd done an excellent job running the center in my absence. Now it was time to put my grief behind me and throw myself into my work.

Hiring seasonal employees like Joe was one of my responsibilities. Around this time, Gulf War veterans were returning, looking for work. I had recently taken a seminar explaining the benefits of hiring war vets and how they could fit into parks and recreation jobs. It was with that encouragement that I hired Tank Reynolds.

Tank was a war stud who had come home and bulked up on good old American food. After a life of MREs, he'd made up for lost time. That's why he assumed his once ripped military physique still fit into his tight biker shorts and a spandex shirt. With a thick Jheri curl on top and the added weight, Tank was an imposing figure. I didn't know how he'd looked in military gear, but I was certain

Iraqi soldiers would've messed their shorts seeing him coming over a sand dune.

Joe and Tank worked together the entire summer, running the camp and handling the field trips. Tank was a hard worker, an easy guy to work with. And he was my first war vet hire. Other than his ill-fitting clothes, he was a solid employee.

One Wednesday in late August, a devastated Tank came into work telling us how someone had broken into his home. "Everything was taken," he cried. "To make matters worse, I was looking forward to wearing my uniform in that big parade they're having this weekend for us Gulf War vets. I can't show up looking like this."

Word spread fast and camera trucks arrived. That night, Tank was all over TV, reluctantly detailing the men he had saved in the war and medals he'd won. Reporters took turns saying what a cruel thing the robbery was, especially for someone who had fought for our freedom and saved lives.

The next morning, an avalanche of people showed up at the rec center, dropping off furniture, clothing, electronics, and money. It came pouring in. I couldn't believe the power of television.

Fortunately, someone fixed up Tank with a uniform and the proper medals so he could march in the parade. The cameras followed his proud journey on the parade route, turning him into a minor celebrity. We were happy for him.

When the dust settled, we looked over all the stuff we'd taken in. I was pretty sure he'd have to sell some of it. After all, no one needed four couches.

The other aspect of this was the amount of money we had received for Tank. Karen totaled it up and the final figure was staggering. When his job ended a week later, I was thrilled he'd be set up for a while—maybe a year or more. It filled my heart to see local citizens supporting our troops and blessing a good person—*a freedom fighter*—like

Tank Reynolds. It also sent a great message to our troops: If you fight for us, we'll take care of you.

A month later, a detective showed up at the rec center. He needed to talk to me and Joe. Apparently, Tank Reynolds had not earned any medals in the Gulf War, mainly because he'd never been out of the country or in any military service. Tank's real name was Karl Johnson, and his actual profession as listed on his social security form was con artist. He'd fooled me and our HR department, along with thousands of citizens. As the detective's lips moved, I ground my teeth into nubs. Thank God I was in a wheelchair, because I wanted to choke the ever-loving life out of Tank—I mean, Karl. Fortunately, I never got the chance.

When they finally caught up with Karl, a judge sent him a different message: If you lie about fighting for us, we'll take care of you. Karl received four years in federal prison for fraud. The detective called it "Stolen Valor." But things worked out for Karl. He received "three hots and a cot," along with several medals as the team leader of cell block D. Oh, and he had to trade in those tight biker shorts and spandex shirt for a white jumpsuit with stripes down the side. He called it "unfair." I called it "justice."

●——●

With summer over, Joe decided to stay on. I had lost my recreation leader, so I promoted Joe to that position. It was a part-time job, which he needed because he was still going to school. I have to say with all the drama, it was nice having a good friend to watch my back.

The area surrounding the rec center was full of gang activity. That's why the rec center was like a beacon—a safe haven—for the kids who wanted to avoid trouble. Two kids we loved spending time with were Joseph and George. These boys were hungry for some attention from stable men. They observed how Joe and I acted and absorbed everything we had to say. I could tell that if they would've been able to select their parents, they would've picked one of us. That's why it was incredibly sad when we learned Joseph had shot himself playing Russian Roulette. Joe and I attended the young boy's funeral and had barely recovered when we learned of another tragedy. George had gotten into a fight with another kid in the apartments around the corner from the rec center. He'd been stabbed to death, which sent us to another funeral. How things like this could happen was beyond my comprehension. Of course, I couldn't understand why my brother was gone at thirty-three.

A few weeks after all this, I found out my parents were getting a divorce. They had been married over thirty-three years. It was another gut punch. I could tell my dad had been struggling for a while, so it wasn't a total surprise.

My father had a painful beginning to life. He was born as a twin, but his parents could only afford to keep one child. It wasn't Dad. They'd given him away to some aunts or cousins to raise. I don't know for sure, but this had to mess with his mind, thinking they loved his sibling and not him. He had to wonder why they didn't choose him. It wasn't a great beginning to Dad's life. Then add in my accident and Chonny's death, and Dad had experienced a lot of pain.

Apparently, Mom and Dad had decided to wait until David graduated college to minimize the effect on him. Divorce is not confined to the parents, after all. The pain spreads to every child, affecting our relationships later in life. I know I felt it, and I'm sure Ninfa and my siblings did too. All we could do was deal with it and move on.

As I said earlier, the area around the rec center was full of gangs. With a junior high on one side and an elementary school on the other, we were stuck in the middle of a war zone.

One day, I sent Joe to city hall to drop off some paperwork. On his way back, he noticed a boy sitting on a three-foot wall in front of our rec center. Checking his watch, Joe realized it was almost three. He came into my office to discuss it.

"Ray, there's this kid outside just sitting there. He's too young not to be in school."

"Okay," I said. "You know some of these kids get suspended. We won't let him in until school lets out and the rest of the kids are allowed in. Maybe that's what he's doing there—waiting for the school bell to ring."

"Yeah, I guess," Joe said, walking back to the front desk.

Twenty minutes later, the schools let out and kids streamed through the front entrance. Every day was like this—a madhouse at this time. That's when I heard the *Pop! Pop! Pop!* of an automatic weapon.

"Get the kids inside!" I yelled to Joe.

He jumped over the desk and ran to the entrance, yanking kids in. I rolled there to help and saw a young boy calmly walking on the rec center grass toward a house across the street. This particular house held the leader of a gang. Each afternoon, this gang leader met up with his buddies to draw up plans for the latest murder, robbery, or drug-related crime. It never stopped.

For some reason, this young kid had taken exception to that and used the opportunity to shoot at the leader and his gang members as they exited their cars. The kid kept shooting until another car pulled up and he got in. Then they drove away as if it was another day in the life of a gangbanger—which it probably was.

The police arrived and performed an investigation, setting out tiny evidence tents near each casing. Incredibly, no one on rec center property had been hit. It was a true miracle. The police took photos of everything, then loaded up their equipment and went home, leaving us to fend for ourselves. For us, it was just another day at the Charley Taylor Recreation Center.

Chapter Fifteen

Since this was my first time leading a rec center, I was fortunate to have skilled experts above me. They spent hours training me to do my job. Ron Neely, my boss, showed me how to create line-item budgets for municipalities. This particular task was more like an art. I had to learn what items to keep in the budget and what to toss out.

Politics played a huge role in budget-making and receiving the requested funds. "If you're in charge of a facility," Ron explained, "you have to sacrifice some needs to make the entire department look better. The politicians can't make your rec center the shiny penny while leaving the other rec centers looking like rundown shacks."

I discovered that I competed against my peers, all of whom wanted to make their centers fresh and modern. If I went in and asked for everything, they might give me only the low-priority items. Instead, the game was to ask for a few high-priority needs with one or two smaller-priced wants. Ron's technique worked well.

I guess I did well enough running the rec center, because a decision was made to add another center to my responsibilities. Truman was a part-time school-based center. This meant that we used a junior high school's gymnasium as the actual center, instead of a separately built facility.

Using buildings that sat empty during non-school hours was a smart move since it gave the kids a place to go when school was out for the day. It also opened on Saturdays, hoping to draw kids there instead of out on the streets where trouble lived.

I drove back and forth to each center, making sure they ran smoothly. My staff and I created a class schedule and hired in the appropriate workers.

I soon found Karen's and Joe's help to be invaluable. They ran Charley Taylor while I was at Truman, and sometimes one of them went to Truman while I stayed at Charley Taylor. We communicated and coordinated who was supervising where. Somehow, it all worked out.

We went on like this day after day and week after week. Many times, after a long week of hustling and hard work, Joe and I drove to a nearby bar to grab a beer. We'd find a semi-clean table in the corner where we could people watch and engage in an endangered activity called "conversation." On one occasion, Joe brought up the wreck.

"Did you ever run in to the guy who was driving you that night?" he asked.

"Sure. Craig showed up at the hospital a few times. He also checked in on me after I was out. I could see he was definitely upset but we both knew that he felt guilty about what happened. His driving put me in this chair. Nothing I can say will ever change that fact. We stay in touch but more like distant friends."

Joe sipped a chilled mug of beer and changed the subject. "You know, I've got you figured out,"

"Oh really?"

"Yeah. Like when I was new and Nancy was still there. We had to get the gym floor swept up because league play was starting in an hour. I came in to grab a broom and there you were, the broom handle between your neck and shoulder, wheeling up and down the gym floor. When I tried to get the broom away from you, you refused.

And you did all this in that short-sleeved business shirt and tie. I was stunned you'd do something like that."

"It had to get done," I said. "I was there, so I did it. It's called management through leadership."

"For sure. That's why I've learned that if something needs to get done, I'd better do it or you're going to beat me to it. Like that recent snowstorm."

"What about it?" I asked, taking a deep swallow of beer.

"I was in bed when you called and said we were delaying the opening of the center. 'Don't try to come in until ten,' you said. I leaned back and closed my eyes to get some bonus sleep. Then it hit me. You were going to work right then. I was sure of it. So I got up and drove through the snow and ice and sure enough, there you were, making your way through the snow trying to get to the building. Man, that was something else. I couldn't decide if I was happier almost beating you to work or knowing I had you figured out."

I grinned. "What can I say? You got me. Now you know how I operate."

Joe chuckled, leaning back in his seat as the condensation from his glass dripped onto the table. "I do. Because the thing with you is this: How can anyone complain about their job when you're outworking us? I mean, you're not going to be making any excuses."

It was funny to hear how one of my subordinates viewed me. I had to admit it was nice to have Joe's respect. Besides being a close friend, he was a hardworking, loyal employee.

●——●

By 1994, my sister, Debbie, had two kids: three-year-old Morgan and four-year-old Dalton. Since Joe didn't have family in town, he spent a lot of time over at our house. As such, I was able to use him to have some fun at my sister's expense.

One evening, we were relaxing inside when Dalton wanted Joe to play with him. Debbie was in the back room, so I couldn't pass up this opportunity.

"Hey, Joe," I whispered. "Tell Dalton to say 'fire truck.'"

"Okay," Joe said, shaking his head. "Hey, Dalton, come here." He put Dalton right in front of him. "Say fire truck."

Dalton yelled the two words loud enough for Debbie to hear. The only problem was, Dalton could not yet make the T sound. Instead, he substituted a letter he was more comfortable with—F.

Debbie came storming into the living room, livid. "Ray, you told!" Then she turned to Joe. "I know Ray told you to do that!"

An embarrassed Joe nodded. Unfortunately, Debbie's anger convinced Dalton he had a hold of something important. That's why he spent the next ten minutes repeating the amended version of fire truck as loud as his little voice could. Debbie finally convinced Dalton to stop. When she calmed down, Joe secretly laughed with me. It was the jokester side of me that most folks never saw.

·———·

There was always action outside the Charley Taylor Recreation Center. The house we had the most problems with sat across the street from the main entrance. One time, the same gang leader who had been the target of the shooting had his guys form up their cars to block traffic. Another caravan of cars stopped fifty yards away, blocking off the other half of the street. This created a car-free zone in front of the rec center. We stood at the front entrance, confused, as the two gangs approached each other and commenced a large brawl. They knew it took five minutes for the police to arrive, so they were determined to get their licks in.

During the fourth minute, someone called time. They collected their injured comrades, shoved them in the cars, and took off. By the time the police arrived, everyone had vanished

A month or two after the gang fight, there was another drive-by shooting nearby. This time, a woman—an innocent bystander—was killed. Police arrested a boy, someone we knew. He used to come to the rec center and play sports. He had just graduated high school and worked a full-time job at the airport. I felt like he was a good kid, so I was completely shocked to find he was headed to prison. It was almost impossible for any kid to grow up normal in this type of environment.

Each time I was outside and heard the *Pop! Pop! Pop!* of an automatic, I'd try to roll as fast as I could up the center's ramp and get inside. If someone was with me, they usually ran ahead to open the door instead of pushing me. Sometimes I think they believed my wheelchair was bulletproof. I was blessed to have never been hit by a round.

Besides violent action, there was a wide assortment of characters in and around the rec center. Chi Chi was one of them. He would come in and play ping-pong. For some reason, he liked me.

Chi Chi was a real character, always hustling something. Sometimes he'd come through there with stolen groceries and other goods trying to peddle them to our clients. I'd have to talk with him and steer him outside. The next time, he'd show up with a thick wad of cash, asking me to go have a beer with him. He also talked with Joe a lot.

I didn't know what Chi Chi did for a living, but I knew he resembled a hardworking farmer because he planted seeds all over town. That's why he had a mess of children with a bunch of women. I told him he should focus on being a good role model for his kids and act like a father. He responded with sad tales of his upbringing and how hard he'd had it.

"You think you have it bad," I told him, "come walk in my shoes for a day."

Chi Chi smiled and said, "No thanks."

"That's what I thought," I said, ending the discussion.

He always had some angle going on. One day, he stopped coming in. We never heard what happened to Chi Chi. Like so many people in the area, he just disappeared.

Anthony and Junior were two more guys we often saw in the rec center. They were young adults, about twenty-one years old, who came in to talk to me and Joe. Really, they were looking for advice and guidance in their lives. I'd listen and try to give them some direction. Joe and I were always there if they needed someone to talk to.

One day, Junior came in with his mouth set in a tight, grim line. He told us Anthony had passed out on some railroad tracks at night. When the train came along, it couldn't stop in time. Anthony disappeared under the wheels. And that was the end of Anthony. Eventually, Junior stopped coming in too.

I had another good friend, Trent, who often came by. I first met Trent early in my career. His children were involved in the Irving Parks and Recreation program that I coached. I became good friends with him through that program.

Trent would do anything for you. He drove a truck and worked hard to support his family. One night, he drove through a snowstorm and his truck broke down. With the engine not working, he couldn't generate any heat. A few days later, his children called to tell me their father had frozen to death in his cab. And that was the end of Trent.

Joe and I attended more funerals than we could count. Teenagers. Boys in their twenties. You name it. Some committed suicide. Others were killed as gang members. I'd listen to the eulogies, which seemed to glorify gang life. Each one who died was a kid Joe and I had tried to counsel and turn around. We had some victories to go with a ton of defeats. It was very sad.

This all happened in Grand Prairie, but it wasn't a bad place to live. There were just a few pockets of deep trouble that stained the entire community. Every city has those places.

—•

Lunchtime at the rec center often found us congregating at a nearby restaurant. Many times, it was just me and Joe. Joe would always buckle up, afraid I might wreck my van in the rush. "You have a lead hand!" he always told me. That was probably true. I wanted to get to where we were going, eat, and get back—fast.

One time, we went to Burger King. Because my wheelchair wouldn't fit between the metal railings, I rolled up to the counter when it was my turn. Some drunken fool took exception to that and made a few sarcastic comments. That's when my bodyguard stepped in.

"You need to go about your business or you'll have a problem," Joe said, invading the man's space. The drunk glanced at me then back to Joe. Deciding he didn't want a piece of Joe, he slinked away.

Joe and I had that kind of relationship. If I had a problem and needed muscle, he was there for me. But Joe was much more than muscle. He could run the center when Karen and I were gone. We were lucky to have him.

After a long week of drive-bys and funerals, we needed some relief. To blow off steam, we'd shut the rec center down and go to a little club nearby. There, we solved all the world's problems.

One night we tried a larger, modern-looking joint. There were plenty of women all over it. I found being confident in a wheelchair drew women like magnets, especially if they'd been drinking. This night, Joe and some other buddies were hanging around me, trying to pick off one or two of them. One girl came up and sat our table, genuinely interested in my condition.

"So, when you have children, will they be in a wheelchair like you?" she asked innocently. The truth was, I *could* have children—as most quadriplegics could. Her question was quite common. Most people are ignorant to that fact. Still, I decided to have some fun.

"No," I replied. "Because I'm not allowed to have children."

"Why not?"

"Because no woman can stand to give birth to a baby in a wheel-chair. The tiny front wheels can make it out, but the larger rear wheels would rip a woman open. She can barely get the head of a baby out. Forget a wheelchair."

Her eyes grew large as she considered what I'd said. Joe, sitting next to me, covered his mouth and tried not to laugh out loud.

"That's too bad," was all she said. A few seconds later, she picked up her drink and left.

Joe saw her leave and told the guys what had just gone down. We laughed about it all night.

At 2 a.m., they turned off the music and the lights clicked on. The party was over.

We went outside to get in the van when Joe and one of our buddies said they had to pee bad. They walked to the rear of the parking lot and stood facing the wall of another building. Soon, they were letting the good times flow. Just as they neared the end, Joe heard someone else peeing. He looked to his right and saw me emptying my bag. I had pulled the plug, which caused the urine to shoot out toward the wall.

"What?" I asked, noticing his incredulous stare. "I had to go too."

Joe started laughing—hard. Decades later, he would tell me that was the moment when he no longer saw the chair. From that point on, he just saw Ray. I was one of the guys then—no different than him.

●—●

Besides supervising two rec centers—Charley Taylor and Truman—I administered a $60,000 budget, which was part of a community development block grant. This gave us the money during the summer to provide free lunches to students or children who lived in the neighborhood around the rec center. They had to qualify first. If they did, they were given a card to come in and get lunch. It wasn't much more than some sandwiches and chips—nothing hot—but it filled their hungry bellies.

Managing money like the block grant led to one of the frustrating things about working in government. I had to spend all of my budgeted money each year. In private business, I could return the money and receive a bonus. Not in this world. If I didn't spend it, I didn't get it next year. It was sometimes wasteful.

For large capital expenditures, we'd have to sell a bond program to the taxpayers and let them decide if we could have the money. This included money for major repairs. With my lower position in the food chain, upper management took care of any bond programs we needed.

To keep on top of industry trends and new ideas, I joined the Texas Recreation and Parks Society. TRAPS is a professional organization that holds local and state conferences. I also joined the National Recreation and Parks Association. NRPA put on national conferences each year. These two organizations really helped me network with others in this industry.

A key part of networking is learning about new opportunities. In early 1995, I heard about a job in Irving. They needed a rec center supervisor for Senter Park. That rec center was 36,000 square feet, larger than my current 12,000 square feet center. And the budget was almost double. Everything about it was bigger, including the salary. I didn't want to jump jobs because Grand Prairie had been so good to me, giving me a chance when no one else would. But I'd been with Grand Prairie for almost five years and felt I'd paid them back handsomely, especially since I'd increased revenues by eighteen percent each year. It was time for me to spread my wings.

I interviewed with Irving's Bill Beavan and Dwight Pinnix. Dwight was the superintendent of recreation. Both men had heard of me and knew I was in a wheelchair. That was huge. They also knew I'd worked for Irving years earlier as a part-time employee. Plus, I had a good reputation, enough for them to feel comfortable. If I was going to move up in this industry, this was as good a shot as I could get.

They questioned me about everything I'd done at Grand Prairie and problems I'd dealt with. After hearing about the two centers I'd managed along with a block grant, they could see I was well qualified. The only question was who I'd be up against.

Like the last job, the wait was long and agonizing. I wanted it badly and I wanted it now.

In early April, I received the call. "Ray, you're the one we picked. Congratulations."

After I hung up, I wanted to jump up and down—but of course I couldn't. One thing I could do was celebrate. I gave my notice and went out with my family and friends for a good time. Then I prepared to place the rec center in Karen's more than capable hands.

I told Joe I wanted him to get Karen's assistant supervisor's job. He agreed to go for it.

When my last day arrived, they threw a party for me. I was excited about the new challenge, but sad because I was leaving the folks who'd given me a shot. As I rolled around Charley Taylor one last time—a place where I knew every nook and cranny—I remembered small incidents. Like when a little kid dropped his snow cone near the softball field and cried, making a big fuss until we got him a fresh one. Or when a basketball game got heated and we had to call the police. Or each time I had to fight my way through the snow to get to the front door. All of these million memories would stay with me, giving me a warm feeling as well as experience to handle some future situation. It was a treasure I took with me.

When the party was over, I received plenty of hugs and well wishes. Then I turned my office over to Karen and rolled down the ramp to my van. It was time to move on.

Chapter Sixteen

For my first day on the job, I arrived early, carrying with me a list of goals I wanted to achieve that day. It included meeting the staff, inspecting the facilities, and reviewing the files. Not ten minutes in, a harried staff member came running up to me. "Mr. Cerda, you're needed in the Advisory Council meeting. They're convening right now."

The Advisory Council was a group of people from the community, volunteers who provided input on the facility and how it was being operated.

"Are you kidding me? I just got here," I said, wondering if this was a prank.

"I know. But this was scheduled months ago, and it just so happens to be your first day."

"First day? It's my first hour," I muttered.

I grabbed a fresh pad of paper and rolled into the meeting room. There, sitting at a U-shaped desk arrangement, were fifteen members of the community. It reminded me of all my past job interviews.

"This is Ray Cerda," the staff member told the group. "He's the new rec center supervisor."

Several members frowned.

"Hi," was all I managed before the barrage of questions came.

"Where are you from?"

"How many years have you been doing this?"

"What kind of experience do you have?"

Clearly, they had been told nothing about me—including the wheelchair part. Because I was replacing a woman who'd been there for twenty-five years in that position, I could sense some anxiety. This would be a challenge. Yet I'd learned to expect the unexpected during my recovery. This was just another test of my abilities. I smiled and dove right in.

They hit me from all angles. I answered their questions, many of which touched on my work ethic and integrity. One even asked what I was going to do to make the rec center better than the woman leaving. I politely explained that since I'd been on the job less than an hour, I'd be more prepared at the next meeting.

About halfway through, I reminded myself of all those years I'd spent with no permanent full-time job. I was grateful to undergo this grilling, because it meant I had a very good job. Those three years had taught me to appreciate whatever work challenges came my way.

When it was over, I thought I'd done fairly well. I had the impression they'd give me a few weeks to achieve everything on their extensive list. With that done, it was time for me to roll up my sleeves.

I grabbed my assistant and went on a tour of the facility. Senter Park was the largest recreational facility in Irving. It had a volleyball and basketball gym, four racquetball courts, a locker room and showers, a fitness room, two classrooms, and an upstairs dance studio. Unlike my last job, there were no outside softball fields or sand volleyball courts.

Toward the end of the tour, I rolled to the outdoor pool and stared at it for a while. This was the exact spot I'd honed my swimming skills, the ones I'd picked up at Glenn's pool. It was like coming back home.

When I finished the tour, I met the staff of twenty-five employees, going over their employment records and any issues they brought to my attention. If they were on contract, I discussed renewals with pay rates and expected work times. Everyone seemed satisfied.

At the end of my first day, I knew I'd love working here. The center had a healthy budget. This gave me more responsibilities, allowing me to make a big difference in the community. And my personality and career fit with Irving. I'd gone to Irving High School and knew many of the folks who used the facility. Plus, the city of Irving was bigger than Grand Prairie. I was the same fish in a bigger pond, working my way up the food chain. It was exciting. I couldn't wait to get home and tell my family all about it.

●——●

After settling in, I was determined to upgrade my facility. One of my first big projects was getting a marquee sign installed on the ground in front of the facility. This type of sign had little plastic letters inside the case. I'd learned about it from the two associations I'd joined—TRAPS and NPRA. Between their monthly magazines and the other facility supervisors I met at the meetings, I'd learned of current trends in the parks and recreation industry and made a list of wants for my center. One of them was that sign. I wanted everyone to know the hours of operation, current activities, and the ones they needed to sign up for. Once installed, it brought in more people, who signed up for more programs and generated even more fees. It was a good start to what I hoped would be a first-class facility.

●——●

In my second year at Senter Park, I reviewed our financials and realized we'd generated enough money from the program fees to put in some goodies. First, I installed a sand volleyball court. Once that was up and running, I redid the existing playground unit. Then I added fitness equipment to the weight room. The fitness equipment and playground unit were nice, but the great thing about having an outdoor sand volleyball court was more leagues. More leagues meant more money from program fees. That increased our revenue. Combined with the money we were already making, I could do more for the facility without having to go through the city and its budgetary process.

My staff and I worked hard to generate fees from everything we did. This included our day camps and afterschool programs. With the revenue increasing, I felt good about the center's future.

Still, I used the budgetary process to add some outdoor amenities, including covered pavilions and picnic tables. These were paid for through the general fund account, which came from the yearly budget requests. Having more people hanging around the outside of the rec center meant more people enjoying the great outdoors—and seeing my sign to enroll in a program.

Speaking of outdoors, Senter Park was not like Charley Taylor Rec Center in Grand Prairie. There weren't frequent drive-bys and gunshots. However, I did have to occasionally call the police. This happened twice a year or so, when a parent failed to pick up their child from our after-school program. Once the police arrived, so did Child Protective Services. They took the kid to a shelter and started a legal process to find out what happened to the parent, which usually meant court, lawyers, and fees.

Another incident involved two kids fighting outside on the premises. I had to go out there and break it up while my staff called the police. Still, this was nothing compared to the Charley Taylor Rec Center.

It was around this time that I had a part-time position open up. Joe Moses had told me he'd just finished college and had his bachelor's degree. While attending night school, Joe had stayed at Grand Prairie as their full-time rec leader. Now that he had his degree, he was promoted to Karen's assistant. Karen had been permanently bumped up to my old job. I was happy for them both, but missed having Joe by my side to help out with things.

"I can't do it," he said when I called him about my part-time opening. "I have a full-time job running the same rec center you used to run. You know what it's like."

I'd assumed he'd say that. "Come on. It's mostly nights and weekends. That's exactly the same time you've been going to school and studying. At least now, you'll be making more money with two jobs."

"I don't know," he said.

"I can work with you on your schedule over there in Grand Prairie."

"You know, you're right!" he said. "I've been going to school during that time, so why not fill the hole in my schedule with money?"

"That's the Joe I know and love." He'd just fallen into my trap. I wanted him to start working for Irving so I could eventually poach him away.

Joe worked part-time at Senter Park for two years. Then he was bumped up to center supervisor of Charley Taylor Rec Center in Grand Prairie. He made great money holding down two jobs. My master plan was working.

———•———

As I said earlier, quadriplegics can and do have children. Many go on to marry and have children. And no, our children are not born into wheelchairs. Knowing this, there was a bright, attractive, kind woman I worked with who took an interest in me. I was attracted to her so we began hanging out, doing things together. Over time, I could see she was falling for me. I had to make another decision.

I reminded myself of how much work it was to take care of me. Ninfa worked hard to tend to my needs in the morning before I left and at night, when I came home. Would my new wife be able to handle everything? And what happened if my new wife discovered it was harder than she thought?

During a long weekend, I pondered all this. The next time I saw her, I said, "I know you are getting serious with me. I can see it in your eyes. But you don't know what's ahead of you. There's too much you'll have to do. You'll have to take care of me. You'll have to get me out of bed. You'll have to shower me. You deserve more."

She started to resist, but I cut her off. "Listen, I've made the decision. I want you to start looking for another guy and stop hanging out with me. I slipped up because I loved spending time with you. But this is it. I have to let you go."

It was a sad moment, one I didn't enjoy experiencing. But it was something I had to do. After that, I remained distant to any woman who tried to get close. For me, it's just the way it had to be.

●——●

There is knowledge you can obtain in college that allows you to do your job. Then there are tasks where college provides a mere sliver of the total amount of knowledge you need to successfully complete them. Experience in the field provides the rest of the needed skills. Obtaining items you want and need for your recreational center through the budgetary process falls under the latter category. Very little you learn in college will help you navigate the rocky shoals of getting a politician to give you taxpayer money. It's both an art and a science.

One of the first tricks I learned was to prioritize my needs. If I needed a new shower and an updated weight room, the shower would be my first request. If each item cost $50,000 and I thought the politicians would only allocate me $75,000, I'd ask for a new shower and a $25,000 resurfacing of the basketball court. If I asked for the new shower and the updated weight room, I would likely get only the shower. The reason was simple: I was competing with my brother and sister rec centers. They each had their wants and needs list. They were trying to snag as much money as they could for their center. It was both a math and a political game, with some guesstimating thrown in. Of course, my supervisor would often help me in this process. He could tell me how much he thought I might get, and then review my list to see if it made sense. He would kick it up to the director to review, who took it to the city council. There, the politics were even more intense. A lot of horse-trading and shenanigans went on.

After experiencing many rounds of this in Grand Prairie and now at Irving, I was pretty confident I knew what I was doing. That's when a surprise entered the process: an influential constituent complaint. If I'd been successful hogging all the money for my rec center, citizens who attended other rec centers would call their council members and complain. Those politicians would jump all over our director of parks and recreation. If it stung him bad enough, that pain could travel downhill back to us. That's why I had to anticipate this and not put myself in a position where I received an uneven percentage of money from the general fund. And, hopefully, my fellow rec center supervisors weren't telling some local citizen, "Gee, I'm sorry that the shower is so crappy, Mr. Jones. Senter Park gets all the money and we get almost nothing. Maybe you could call your council member and complain? Wait, here's her number."

The good news for me was our yearly increasing revenues. As I invested in new money-making additions, I left the budgetary process for non-revenue-generating items like new showers and resurfacing the basketball court. Sure, a nice shiny floor made the basketball players happy. But it didn't necessarily make the center more money. Adding my sand volleyball court did.

I had to admit it was fun being the CEO of a business while playing the math and political games to win. If I didn't like it, I could always go back to rolling around for three years looking for a job.

—•—

After Joe had been working part-time for me for two years, it was time to spring the trap. One day, I picked up the phone. "Hey, Joe, a position just opened up for West Park Rec Center supervisor. Why don't you go for it?"

"I don't know, Ray. I'm making good money working both jobs. With no time to spend it, I've got a nice savings account. I'm not applying for that. I'm already rec center supervisor here in Grand Prairie."

I'd assumed he'd say that. "But dude, with the salary they're offering, you'll make almost as much doing the one job, and you won't be running around doing all that stuff you do now. You can't go on like this forever. You'll break down."

"That makes sense," he said, hesitating. "You know, I'll throw my name in the hat."

The toss was excellent, because his name came out of that hat. Suddenly, I had my good buddy on the Irving team. I wanted to jump for joy—but of course, I couldn't.

—•—

As in Grand Prairie, I established a fun lunch "gang" to hang out with. Almost every day, we'd go somewhere for lunch, spreading out over two or three tables. We'd tell jokes, talk about sports, exchange knowledge and stories, and carry on for an hour until we had to get back to work. A lot of informal mentoring went on over lunch. This time was a thrill for me, because I felt like an equal when everyone was seated. It was one of the highlights of my day.

One of the things we spoke about at lunch touched on a town hall meeting Joe and I were going to attend. Everyone would be there. Directors. A city manager. Politicians. Movers and shakers. And one homeless man named Dilly-Day. None of us knew Dilly-Day before this day, but that was about to change.

The building set for the meeting was the Hispanic Chamber of Commerce. It was small—really too small for what was about to go down.

Joe and I arrived early and found a spot away from the action. We were low men on the totem pole. It was our job to observe and listen, not speak.

No sooner had I parked my wheelchair than Dilly-Day began making all sorts of noise. Joe leaned forward, trying to understand what he was saying, but like me, he couldn't make out a coherent thought.

I glanced around the room and saw no one was paying any attention to him. Joe whispered, "Man, that guy's high out of his mind."

"Really?" I asked.

"Yeah. Just watch him, bro."

Right on cue, an officer strolled in. He approached Dilly-Day, telling him he needed to leave. Directly behind him, a woman from the Hispanic Chamber of Commerce spoke up. "Leave him alone. I pay rent here and I want this guy in this meeting. I'm going to buy him something to eat." She took Dilly-Day in the back somewhere out of sight and the crisis was over.

I heard she went to McDonald's and bought him some food. Meanwhile, the building started filling up. Just as the meeting was about to start, Dilly-Day reappeared from the back and found a chair, holding a McDonald's sack filled with aromatic fries and Quarter Pounder. The smell made me hungry.

I watched as several people around Dilly-Day glanced at his bag of food. I imagined they were contemplating snatching that bag and shoving a fistful of golden fries down their gullet. I know I was.

Apparently, Dilly-Day considered this possibility. Or he might have been commanding the smells back into the bag. Or he might have indulged in a side of shrooms before he'd made it to McDonald's.

Whatever the reason, he started yelling. As people stared at him, he went crazy. The psilocybin or mescaline or methamphetamine kicked in and he went full on *Alien vs. Predator.*

The single officer—the one who'd tried to make sure this situation didn't happen—called for backup. Everyone cleared the building through the emergency side doors except me, Joe, the officer, and Dilly-Day. Being in a wheelchair, I needed to roll down the handicapped ramp. Unfortunately, the building had only one accessible entranceway, and Dilly-Day stood blocking it. Joe, the loyal friend, wasn't going to abandon me.

Helpless, I sat there watching as more officers appeared and tried to calm Dilly-Day down. Like a violent tornado, the crazy fool grabbed one of the officers and a wrestling match broke out. Dilly-Day was like the Predator. He had two officers on the floor fighting, scratching, and punching. Suddenly, one of the officers lost his gun and it came sliding toward us. Then a side pouch of bullets spilled—all of this was inches away from us. Joe and I found we were unwilling patrons attending a WWE event where real weapons were used.

One of the officers freed himself from the dogpile and jammed his Taser against Dilly-Day's chest. A crackling sound preceded a stiff, jerking Dilly-Day. His eyes rolled around as he turned into the Alien, knocking the Taser from the officer and sending it spinning in front of us, joining the growing collection of weapons. A few baton love taps and several more tasings from another officer slowed Dilly-Day down. Just as he was about to make a third run, maybe turn into Godzilla, multiple handcuffs appeared and ended the match. The three officers had won.

Barely.

After the officers collected their bullets and weapons, they escorted an angrily resisting Dilly-Day out, accidentally banging his head on the door jamb, the door, and then the floor. With the disruption over, the politicians canceled the meeting. I never saw that kind woman again—the one who'd insisted on letting Dilly-Day remain for the meeting. I also have no idea what happened to that steaming bag of fresh McDonald's food that Dilly-Day left behind. (If that kind lady had just bought him a Dilly Bar from Dairy Queen or a Bud Light, perhaps we would've never had that outburst. Of course, it's all speculation anyway.)

●——●

I'd been the rec center supervisor of Senter Park for over eight years when upper management decided to do away with the position of rec center supervisor—my position. There were eight rec centers and, thus, eight supervisors. They decided as people quit or retired, they'd heap two rec centers onto one person. The new position would be called Community Program Supervisor, and it came with a raise.

Recently, the supervisor of Lively Pointe had quit, and that center would be added to whoever landed the new position. I studied the criteria and had no choice but to go for it. When I heard Joe was putting his name in the hat too, I realized I'd have to beat out my good friend to move up the food chain. I wondered if I could. And if so, would our relationship change?

I knew one thing: change was coming, and I'd better be ready for it.

Chapter Seventeen

The interview with Dwight Pinnix was intense. I hadn't given one in over eight years and felt a little rusty. On the other hand, I had an excellent track record of running Irving's largest rec center. Handing that over as exhibit one gave me confidence. It was my biggest sales point.

I was up against Joe and two other applicants. I made sure Dwight knew what he had with me. I told him I could make Lively Pointe perform as well as Senter Park. Dwight Pinnix had been with Irving forever, and as recreation manager, he knew every nook and cranny of the division. I hoped I'd done enough to win the position.

After each candidate interviewed, we compared notes to see which way the wind was blowing. When the dust finally settled and the word came down, I received the promotion. Joe was the first to congratulate me.

"You were really their only choice," he said.

Our relationship wouldn't change one bit.

As I drove home, it felt like I'd won a playoff game. Once again, I celebrated with my family. It was always fun to do that.

•———•

Lively Pointe was the fourth largest rec center in Irving. It was a teens-only facility that opened Monday through Friday at four p.m. when school was out and closed at ten p.m. It also had regular hours on Saturday. With Senter Park and Lively, it was exactly like the situation I had handled in Grand Prairie when I'd supervised Charley Taylor and Truman. The new setup kept me driving back and forth, which put me outside. When it was warm, I loved being outdoors.

Working with teens had its own set of challenges. One afternoon, this seventeen-year-old started acting up. I made the decision to remove him from the facility and waited at the door as he was escorted out. When he spotted me, he came up with clenched fists, wearing an angry scowl and yelling, "I'm going to break your [expletive] legs!"

"Bring it on!" I yelled back. "Just stick with the legs because I can't feel anything from the waist down. Who knows? Maybe you'll fix something."

This stunned him. Fortunately, two of my employees held him back, while another employee called the nearby school resource officer. In seconds, the police arrived and took him to a secure facility that had its own kind of rec center—though much smaller.

There was always something going on at Lively.

———•———

About a year into the new position, they handed me Lee Park Center, the third largest rec center. One day, I woke up to supervise three of the top four rec centers in Irving. I now controlled a total budget of close to $1 million and thirty-three employees. Not bad for a quad in a chair.

After several months of running two rec centers, upper management wanted to add programming to Lively Pointe to fill in the early hours when no one was there. Rather than create something new, we pulled the Special Needs Program from West Park and installed it in Lively from nine a.m. to two p.m. This gave us two hours to clear things out before the teen tidal wave hit at four.

The Special Needs Program was a therapeutic program for kids with autism, Down syndrome, mental challenges, and anyone who had a need. We took them on field trips, worked on their life skills, and taught them sports such as basketball, volleyball, softball, and swimming. The parents never said anything, but I could see it in their eyes: "Hey, this guy's in a wheelchair and running this facility. I want my child to see that."

Because I sat in a chair, I was at their eye level. This gave me some connection. When they touched my chair, they knew I was different just like they were. We were different, but the same.

Twenty kids participated in this program. Working with them always put a smile on my face and certainly removed any bad mood I was in.

•——•

By now, Debbie had a third child, Connor. I loved watching him waddle around in his diapers and drool spit, especially when the Dallas Cowboys played on television. He looked like a lineman all hunched over. Of course, he may have been filling up his diaper. It was hard to tell from his facial expression.

The funny thing about kids is what they don't know. Racism is a good example. When I was a child, I hung out with mostly white friends. They didn't see me as different. Only when they had someone over who didn't know me did I have problems. These "strangers" noticed my brown skin and treated me like a second-class citizen. Sometimes I'd be introduced as Italian, as if my nationality was an important part of identifying me. "This is Ray, the Italian." I was sure I was excluded from some events and parties due to my race. It was yet another obstacle I had to overcome.

Joe continued hanging out with my family. They considered him family anyways. We didn't see race or skin color. We just saw a great friend.

One time, my favorite brother-in-law was over, spilling the beans about my younger days. Joe egged him on. "Come on, Jimmy, tell me another Ray story."

"Okay, I have a good one," Jimmy said. "One evening in the hot tub, Raymundo told me that even as a young kid, Ray wanted nice things. He was very fashion conscious. The problem was that they had an old station wagon with no air conditioning. As they approached the school, Ray ordered his father to roll up the windows because he didn't want anyone to know they lacked A/C. If it was hot outside, the station wagon became a sweat box for the few minutes it took to drop off Ray. As soon as Raymundo let Ray out and turned the corner, he rolled the windows down and could start breathing again."

Joe howled with laughter. "That's just like Ray. He's always looking at the new models of chairs and vans. He's got to be in style."

"I'm glad you can all laugh at my expense," I said.

Debbie, laughing too, said, "I still haven't forgiven you over making Dalton say fire truck."

Family. You can pick your nose and you can pick your seat, but you can't pick your family.

◆———●

I was working in my office at Lee Park one day when a lady brought her daughter to a class. She went up to the front desk and asked who ran this rec center. When the front desk employee told her, "Ray Cerda," the woman covered her mouth and hustled her daughter to class. A few minutes later, I left the facility and went back to Senter Park.

Two days after this incident, I was back at Lee Park when this same woman brought her daughter in again. This time, she asked to see me. When I rolled out, I saw it was a special person in my life: Nancy Brown. The woman who'd given me my big break in Grand Prairie.

We hugged each other and visited for a while. Each time she brought her daughter in, we visited if I was there. I loved showing her the fruits of what she'd started. And I still owe her big time!

•——•

In 2005, Hurricane Rita hit Houston. This was a few weeks after Hurricane Katrina had devastated New Orleans, pushing a mass of humanity west toward Houston. It was a double-dipper of trouble.

To flee Rita, authorities down there evacuated thousands of citizens to the DFW area. Senter Park opened up as one of the designated shelters. This put me and my staff to the test.

The Red Cross helped organize it, but my staff were the boots on the ground. To take care of these folks, we reorganized our schedules, moving programs to other recreation centers. We had my center open 24/7 for twenty straight days, feeding 350 people breakfast, lunch, and dinner. It was a huge undertaking.

Newspaper articles told the story, so much so that people arrived donating all sorts of items. TV crews were there almost every day, interviewing the evacuees. As they spoke, I saw the anxiety and depression they suffered up close. So many of them had lost everything. It was devastating to see.

We put in many extra hours to ensure their comfort. Seeing others in distress made me grateful for what I had.

When it was all over, we were recognized by the city council for the outstanding job we'd done. Another newspaper article and it was back to work.

•——•

A few years after I was made Community Program Supervisor, Joe was up for the same position and Dwight Pinnix gave it to him.

Now Joe supervised both West Park and Northwest. Of course, we celebrated by driving somewhere in my van.

By this time, my second van was getting old. I had traded in the first van—the one Joyce Read had snagged from Frank Parra Chevrolet—and retrofitted a second one. As I looked at new vans, I saw the prices had gone up. The van itself cost about $25,000, and the retrofit another $25,000. Just think of buying two cars at once. On a Community Program Supervisor's salary, it wasn't easy. But by the grace of God, I managed.

One thing I did spend a little money on was motorcycle conversions. Believe it or not, I had a motorcycle that I loved riding. It was a converted motorcycle with the bars fixed and a platform on the side that allowed me to drive it from my wheelchair. Imagine seeing some guy in a wheelchair on the side of a motorcycle flying down the highway with no one holding on to the handlebars. That was me. I drove it on the weekends so I could feel the wind in my hair. For some reason, I had a need for speed.

When I first got the motorcycle, it took a lengthy sales pitch to convince Jimmy to ride it with me. In fact, Jimmy went on one of my first rides—just as I was getting used to the speed and control. During the ride, I took a corner a little too fast and almost hit a tree. Jimmy decided one trip was enough. I didn't blame him. He had three kids to raise.

Eventually, I'd saved up enough money for a down payment on a new home. Lots in Coppell (a city just north of Irving) were being sold and I found one I liked. I selected a builder, who worked with me on the design. I made sure every door and opening was handicapped accessible. With wide open bathrooms, lever knobs, a roll-in shower, reachable light switches, raised sinks, and almost no carpet, the house turned out perfect. Adding the ramps at all the entrances was the final touch. Now all I needed were people to fill it up.

Ninfa had her own room, one that was comfortable and private. After my mother sold her Irving house on Beacon Hill, I convinced her it made sense to move in with me. I wanted to keep an eye on her. Besides, it was about time I started paying her back for all she'd done for me.

Coppell was a great place to live. My brother David lived nearby. So did Debbie and Jimmy. They raised their children in the Coppell school system. I loved being close to their kids because I was like a wise old uncle. They often sought me out for advice.

Since I didn't have kids, I "adopted" them as my own, pouring in what knowledge and experience I'd accumulated. To me, they were the best-looking kids around and I'm not being partial... well, maybe a little bit.

With a new home that made it easy to get around and family living with me and nearby, I was one blessed man. That's why I kind of freaked out when I learned that Dwight Pinnix announced his retirement. Dwight had been with Irving longer than I'd been alive (well, almost). For over thirty-two years, he'd been Recreation Superintendent, then Recreation Manager when they changed the title. Dwight leaving Irving's recreation department was like Superman hanging up his cape. Or Batman shutting down the Batcave. It just didn't happen.

After I pinched myself to make sure this announcement was real, I realized his position was open. Someone would have to fill it. Why not me?

I dreamed about being Recreation Manager in the deep crevices of the night. It was the pinnacle of my career mountain. If I could land this job, I'd be unbelievably satisfied that I had come from a frozen corpse in a rotating bed to running the entire recreation department for Irving. The budget I'd control and the people I'd supervise were big numbers. Since this job opened only once in a person's lifetime, it was like a head football coach finally making the Super Bowl at the end of his career. I had one chance to win. I'd better not blow it.

I sat down and established a game plan as to how I'd get this job. Once again, I listed out my accomplishments. But I needed more. I had to come up with a vision for how I'd be able to go from running the day-to-day operations of three recreation centers to managing an entire division. I had been out in the field all my career. This position would put me in city hall. I needed to dazzle the person making the decision.

When I hear people say God doesn't exist, I know they're wrong. All I have to do is point to this example. When I graduated from high school and needed a summer job, I went to the Irving Parks and Recreation Department and saw a position open for a summer assistant track coach. I applied for it. And who interviewed me? You can look back at Chapter Ten or take my word for it: Chris Michalski. He was an administrator in the parks and recreation department. He'd given me the job—my first as a handicapped person.

And guess who'd climbed the ranks to become the parks and recreation director? Chris Michalski.

Last but not least, guess who would be interviewing me and deciding if I landed this job? Yep. Chris Michalski!

I had one shot in my career for a job like this, and a man who knew me well was at the helm making the decision. Still, I left nothing to chance.

My interview with Chris was fantastic. He knew my life story, my career, where I'd worked, and everything about me. I was up against five highly qualified applicants, including Joe. Incredibly, I won. I could hardly believe it. The extra salary would come in handy to pay for a new van and expenses on my house. Of course, this meant a big celebration. And my family knows how to celebrate.

Joe attended the celebration. Hands on his hips, he had something to get off his chest. "I just can't get rid of you. First, you're my boss in Grand Prairie, and now you're my boss here. What's up with that?"

I grinned. "If you would've landed this job, I would've been working for you."

"And trust me, you would've loved that," Joe said as a grin threatened to turn into a smile. "I would've been a great boss, just like you're going to be to me. Right?"

"Right!"

We laughed before grabbing a beer and celebrating all night long.

When I finally came back down to Earth, it was time to roll up my sleeves and get to work. I knew with Chris Michalski's age and abilities, he wasn't going anywhere for a long time. Chris was not only responsible for parks and recreation, he oversaw the libraries as well. That shows how much confidence Irving had in him. Since he had so much to do and I would retire in this position, I wanted to take the recreation department off his worry list. This meant I needed to up my game big time.

The city paid for me to get some additional education. I took courses in Lean Six Sigma, earning my green belt. Tommy Gonzales, the City Manager, was very instrumental in pushing all department heads to learn this information.

The goals behind Lean Six Sigma were to eliminate waste and reduce variation to increase performance. For example, if we put on a program that had only three people attending, that facility could be better used with another program that brought in more people. When we ordered equipment, spending that extra time with team members to ensure we didn't overbuy supplies and equipment was critical. If we did, not only were we wasting money, but we'd have to store it until we could find a use for it.

A lot of this might seem fundamental, but when you're running a facility and dealing with the daily crush of problems, it's easy to lose sight of the nickels and dimes walking out of the building. Every nickel we saved meant the city council could send that money to firefighters and police. We were part of a big organization and needed to pay attention to every detail because it mattered.

To receive a green belt, I had to implement a project. I chose to focus on the registration process for classes at our rec centers. We'd always done it by hand, holding it in the gymnasium. If you wanted to sign up for a Monday class, you got in the Monday line. If you wanted to do the Tuesday classes, you got in the Tuesday line. There were times where our customers didn't get in any of the classes. They signed up for Wednesday classes only because they couldn't get in the Monday and Tuesday classes. The lines were way too long.

Our antiquated registration also caused errors, which led to dissatisfied customers. The whole thing reminded me of a frantic college registration. I decided it was time to automate the entire process.

I put a pencil to it and discovered currently, the entire process cost us about $50,000 in staff time for all the rec centers, and we did it four times a year. This didn't include tying up the gymnasium for a day. I found some software and paid $65,000 to implement it and train the staff. Overnight, the registration took less than a few minutes online. No more driving to the rec center and camping out in line. This simple idea saved the city $200,000 per year. And we had a gymnasium we could program for that time. Not only did I earn my green belt, but I received an award from the program and then was asked to make a presentation to a city council work session. That was interesting and fun.

Before Lean Six Sigma, I'd been focused on increasing revenue. Adding dollars to the bank account allowed me to buy new revenue-generating equipment and facilities for the rec center. Now I had a second focus: eliminating waste and waiting times. Every dollar saved was no different than a dollar made through revenue. It's like football. Playing on offense and generating revenue is sexy, exciting, and flashy. But defense is the flip side. Every yard saved is another yard the offense doesn't have to gain.

With my new outlook, I became a dollar-saving hawk. I was determined to leave my job in ten to fifteen years better off than I'd found it.

Speaking of football, Debbie and Jimmy's youngest child, Connor, was playing for Coppell High School. At every game, there was a proud uncle sitting in a wheelchair rooting him on. He played tight end and tackle, and seemed to have the hang of it. Plus, he was a good athlete. That helped.

At most public sporting events, sections are cut into the bleachers for seats for handicapped people in wheelchairs. Usually, these areas have good clean sight lines for all the action. There aren't many advantages to being in a wheelchair, but seats at sporting events is one of them.

Another advantage is handicapped parking spots. Unfortunately, there's a lot of handicapped fraud out there. People hang the blue tags from their mirrors to get closer to the store or restaurant. Instead of parking 100 feet away and enjoying some much-needed exercise, they take up a spot that someone like me actually needs. If they aren't taking the actual spot, they're parking way too close to a handicapped spot. This makes it hard for me to lower the ramp and get out of my van. I truly pray you don't have to become handicapped to understand how hard it is to park more than 100 feet away in a deserted part of the lot, lowering the ramp then dodging cars backing out or racing down the aisles. Being in a wheelchair and low to the ground means many times, they can't see me. It's dangerous for someone like me. Handicapped people are the last ones who need to be in another accident.

This leads me to one of the many stories I have about handicapped parking. One day, I was headed to a store inside a mall to pick up a much-needed part for my wheelchair. The store was located in a remote corner of the mall on the second floor (thank God for elevators!). I drove to the nearest entrance and found a shiny new Lamborghini taking up two handicapped spots—sideways! I thought I'd seen everything, but apparently I hadn't.

As I sat in my van contemplating all this, a security officer in a cart drove right by and did nothing about the Lamborghini. Since the officer didn't care about this illegal act, he wouldn't care about anything I did.

Carefully, I positioned my van close to the Lamborghini without touching it. This allowed me to get out while effectively blocking him in. As I rolled to the mall entrance, a man came shooting out of the building in a distressed manner.

"Hey, man!" he yelled. "You just blocked me in."

"You're parking in a handicapped spot—*man*. I just happened to be handicapped. Are you?"

"Of course not. I didn't want anyone to ding my new car."

"So you put me at risk of injury instead? You do this all the time?"

He frowned and looked away. "No one was parked there and I'm an engineer working here. My firm is inspecting the garage. You know, to keep it safe and all—for people who park, including *handicapped* people."

"Okay," I said. "Thanks for keeping us safe." I resumed my trip to the store.

"Where are you going?" he asked, running in front of me.

"I'm going into the mall. I've got to pick up some things."

"How long are you going to be?" he asked, panic taking hold of his face.

"I don't know. Maybe an hour, two hours."

"An hour or two? Dude, I haven't got time for that."

"Do you think I have time to sit here and wait for you to move your car so I can park?"

He didn't say anything.

Suddenly, the worthless security guard arrived. "Sir," he said to me, "I'll handle this. I'll talk to him. He shouldn't be parking there."

"Freaking A right, he shouldn't be parking there. Let's just call the police to sort this out. In fact, I'm calling the I-Team on CBS." I pulled out my cell phone and began dialing.

"No! Pluuuzzzeeee," the engineer whined. "What can I do to make this up for you?"

"Apologize, then swear you'll never park in another handicapped spot again."

"I apologize, sir. Really. And I'll never park in a handicapped spot again. I swear."

I rolled back, got in the van, and moved it. He carefully backed out and tore out of there, likely trying to spray whatever gravel there was on the asphalt onto my van. Not very professional. The whole event wasted thirty minutes of my time. And all for some guy's selfishness.

Please don't let that be you.

———•———

Life at the Irving Recreation Department was rocking right along. I had a great group of Community Program Supervisors, and Joe was one of them. With the first budget proposal in my new position coming up, I met with my staff to get prepared. I'd been on the job about eight months and wanted this to go smoothly. My boss, Chris Michalski, called me into his office a week before the city council had to review our requests.

"Ray, I'm going to be out of town on a family vacation during budget presentation time. I need you to make it for me."

"Me?" I asked, shocked. "You want me to make the presentations?"

"Yes. You're well-qualified and confident. I feel you'll do the best job. Try to get us everything we're asking for."

"Send me in, coach," I said. "Don't worry. I'll take carry of it."

"I'm sure you will," Chris said.

I prepared like nothing before. No stone was left unturned. No questions or objections were unanticipated.

On the appointed day, I went over the PowerPoint presentation, answering all of their questions. They said they'd discuss it and send me a copy of what they approved.

Back at the office, everyone wanted to know how I'd done. "Pretty good, I think."

I was wrong. They slashed so many items with red ink that they had to call the blood bank and get more red. It was bad. I shuddered to think what Chris would say when he returned from vacation. I knew he'd never let me handle another budget presentation again, that's for sure.

Chris returned Monday and reviewed the cuts. They were deep and wide. This was 2012 and the economy was still recovering from the Great Recession. Texas is a property tax state. Since we have no income tax, local government is funded through property taxes. With folks still licking their wounds, property values were down and payments lagged. Cities had to make tough choices. With firefighters and police at the top of the priority list, parks and recreation were near the bottom. Chris was going to have to make do with much less.

Four days later on a Thursday afternoon, the managing director asked me if I would call the entire parks and recreation administrative team in for a meeting at three p.m. The team, including me, wondered what was going down. Whatever it was, it didn't sound good.

We all stood around a large table (except for me) as the managing director delivered the news. "Chris Michalski just submitted his resignation, effective immediately. We need an interim director of parks and recreation, so we've decided to appoint Ray Cerda to fill that position."

I felt a breeze as ten heads twisted to stare at me. The managing director continued.

"We aren't going to be posting that job for six to eight months. I expect all of you to assist Ray in whatever he needs to properly administer his duties. That is all."

I received some pats on the back, but mostly everyone stooped down to collect their jaws from the floor. I know mine was down there.

No more than five minutes after the announcement, I was in my office staring at my computer screen. The parks and recreation department had 370 full-time, part-time, and seasonal employees with an annual budget of $18 million. It also handled aquatics, special events, parks, athletics, the golf division, and business administration. This was massive—one of the largest departments in the city of Irving. After a few minutes of staring at my computer screen, I shook my head and started laughing.

Are you kidding me? I said to myself.

Thirty years ago, I'd rolled into this building and interviewed for a summer assistant track coach position—a seasonal employee, the lowest of the low. Now, I was running the entire parks and recreation department.

How does this happen?

The answer was clear: God.

Chapter Eighteen

Now that I was temporarily installed as the director of parks and recreation, I needed to up my game. Calling on my college education, Lean Six Sigma training, and concepts I'd picked up in the last ten years, it was time to conduct a SWOT analysis of the entire department.

SWOT stands for Strengths, Weaknesses, Opportunities, and Threats. By thoroughly reviewing every nook and cranny of the department, we were able to determine several issues that needed attention. A weak economy and reduced federal and state funding would make further cuts and reductions necessary. We also had an aging workforce. If we didn't start training their replacements right now, we would have a big problem on our hands.

The opportunities we identified were adding revenue-generating activities to our parks and public trails. More fun runs kept our staff hopping while bringing in much-needed revenue.

Conducting the SWOT analysis had another purpose: It put me in contact with each manager in the parks department, most of whom I didn't know. I learned more about aquatics, parks, and athletics while meeting dozens of lower-level employees. This exercise also opened my eyes to some threats to my own career.

Not everyone was happy with my promotion. First, I was Hispanic. Sure, there might be some lingering racism out there. I expected that.

I was also in a wheelchair. How could someone like me run a department that involved so much physical activity?

Potentially, I had two strikes against me.

Perhaps because of this, or maybe because I was in their way, I soon felt that certain people wanted me to fail. Whispers reached my ears:

"Did Ray turn in that assignment on time?"

"What are his budget skills like?"

"Does he even have the skills *or* experience for a job this important?"

I heard that some people felt I'd been promoted because I was friends with upper management. It was complete nonsense. It also demeaned the managers who promoted me.

Sure, it helped to know people. But did they think upper management wasn't going to do what was best for the city of Irving? If not, they'd be risking their own jobs. It's one thing to know someone. It's another to promote an incompetent friend.

Another hurdle I faced was the fact that I'd come up through recreation, not the parks side. This was a switch from previous years and promotions.

One afternoon, an employee told me another employee was trying to trip me up. I chuckled. "He picked the wrong dude. After all, I'm in a wheelchair. Good luck tripping that!"

I told everyone, "You know what? I wasn't the director here for the past thirty years. I'm going to do what's best for the department and make sure everyone receives an equal opportunity to apply for these positions. The best person will be selected."

I dove in hard and learned all I could about the parks department. This translated into large blocks of hours, not only in my office reviewing endless reports, but in the field laying my hands on the assets and learning about the problems up close. Late-night meetings ate up a lot of my family time.

One person who didn't doubt my abilities was Tommy Gonzales, the city manager. He treated me no differently than anyone else. And he certainly didn't care if I was in a wheelchair.

As I got to know him, I found him to be an excellent city manager. Tommy pushed all of us to do better and save money. We even won the Malcolm Baldrige award—one of the first municipalities to receive it. It showed how efficient we'd become as a city government.

My workload was heavier because I had to do two jobs for the price of one. They weren't replacing me in my old job as recreation manager. As always, my best buddy Joe Moses jumped in to help me out. Anytime I needed him to tackle a problem, he jumped right in. Of course, he still had his normal duties to manage.

After the initial announcement, Joe and I went out to celebrate. He understood like I did that this was an eight-month trial. If I didn't cut it, I'd be back in my old job or gone. I was determined not to let that happen.

The more I worked at my new job, the more I appreciated how much Chris had been handling. It was a tremendous workload. Adding in the duties of my old job, I didn't see much free time.

Since I wasn't the permanent director, I took a more practical approach to budget requests. I fully understood that if they wanted to cut out my maintenance budget, they'd cut it out. There wasn't much I could do about it.

Sure, I would fight for the things and respectfully disagree, but ultimately, it was their decision. So long as I had a fair opportunity to make my case, I was fine with the results.

I learned with Tommy that I could go back and have an offline discussion about certain cuts with him. He could put the items back in the budget if he wanted to.

Despite working hard, I continued to have Monday morning quarterbacks questioning my every move. It came with the territory.

During meetings, I gave these "quarterbacks" a chance to say something, and they never had anything to say. Nevertheless, I continued rolling forward undeterred.

I considered myself a combination of change agent and adapter. A good example is when we were short of manpower to mow our parks due to budget cuts. I adapted by changing the mowing cycle from seven days to every fourteen days. It was *my* job to do *my* best with the parks and recreation I had, not the parks and recreation I wished I had.

During those eight long months, they began a nationwide search for a permanent director. I had an interview with the managing director and the community resources director, answering all of their questions.

"Where do you see the department in five years?"

"You've been doing this position on an acting basis. What things would you change?"

"What things would you not change?"

"What do you see is your legacy?"

They examined my work ethic, my character, and my commitment. At the end of the process, the managing director came and told me I had earned the permanent position. It was a joyous relief—my own personal Super Bowl victory.

I knew I needed good people around me, so I had my old job reclassified as an assistant director position. Then I interviewed all applicants for the job. When I was done, Joe Moses stood head and shoulders above everyone else. And I knew I could absolutely trust him.

A few months after my permanent promotion, Tommy placed me in charge of the Irving Advisory Committee on Disabilities. This committee consisted of nine members, eight of whom were citizens appointed by the city council with the mayor's approval. If someone had any issues within the city of Irving relating to disabilities, those issues would be brought before this board and we'd discuss them.

For example, if someone went into a building and the door wasn't wide enough, they'd submit the problem to us. We'd decide if there was a problem and, if so, how to rectify it. The committee was an important vehicle for disabled citizens to have a voice.

My first meeting as head of the committee was quite interesting. After everyone was seated, I introduced myself to the other eight members. Before I'd launched into the agenda, one of the women on the board seemed irritated with me. I wondered if she thought she should be running the committee. Clearly, she wasn't happy with my appointment.

To face the matter head on, I turned to her and said, "Is everything okay?"

She folded her arms and glared at me. "What makes you qualified to run this Advisory Committee on Disabilities?"

Thinking this was some ill-mannered practical joke, especially since this woman was able-bodied, I glanced at the other seven members—most of whom had horrified expressions on their faces. That's when I realized it wasn't a joke. This lady was actually steamed at me.

I took a deep breath in the suddenly silent conference room and exhaled slowly. Then I let her have it. "Ma'am, have you ever been in a wheelchair when it's pouring down rain, and you can't get into your vehicle because somebody parked too close to you? Have you ever experienced that?"

"No," she said.

"Have you ever experienced falling out of your wheelchair, and you don't have anyone to help you get back into it? Have you ever had *that* problem happen to you?"

"No, sir, I have not," she replied, her anger subsiding.

"Have you ever been in a wheelchair and gotten stuck in an elevator, and the only way you can get out is going downstairs? Have you ever experienced *that*?"

Her words were barely audible. "No, I have not."

"I've been in this wheelchair for thirty years. I think I have more qualifications than you—wouldn't you agree to that?"

She nodded and looked down, saying absolutely nothing the rest of that meeting.

After the meeting ended, several members came up and apologized. "I'm sorry for the way she treated you."

Another said, "I don't know what she was thinking, man."

As for me, I was in disbelief. Once again, I'd been challenged and forced to stake out my authority. Being handicapped, I never knew what obstacles the day might bring.

Each year, we held a disability week to bring awareness to issues people like me faced. Somehow, I convinced our city manager, Tommy Gonzalez, to get in a wheelchair for an entire day. I wanted him to go to work, get in and out of the car, go to restaurants, get in elevators, and then give a talk on it a few days later.

He listed out the problems he'd encountered, saying it was certainly an eye-opening experience. As for me, I was grateful that someone in his position had taken up my challenge and learned a different perspective.

Besides being head of the Disability Committee, I led the Tree Advisory Board, Parks and Recreation Board, Senior Advisory Council, and Youth Council. All of these groups gave citizens a path to tell us what they felt about how we were doing with their parks and rec centers. We learned a lot by listening to their concerns. Sometimes, though, like with the Disability Committee, the volunteers appointed to the board lost their perspective. Some even lost their cool. A rare one or two lost their minds.

There was one board chairman who was upset when I altered his board's vision statement. I happened to be recovering after a hospital stay when he burst into my office, demanding to see me.

"He's not here," my secretary told him. "He's recovering at home from recent surgery."

"I'm going to send him back where he came from!" the man spat out.

"What did you say?" my secretary asked.

"He's going to wish he was back where he's been the past couple of weeks," the man said.

My secretary made notes as the man continued.

"I'm going to do some damage and make him feel worse."

I read the report conducted by the city and was dumbfounded. When he said he was going to send me back to where I came from, did he mean Mexico? I was born in Texas. Maybe he didn't know that.

And the part about doing damage to make me feel worse—dude, I'm a quadriplegic. It's hard to go much further down than that.

The city banned him from talking to any city employee except Joe Moses. Eventually, that was lifted. But that incident was an extreme example of how my ladder to success was different than others.

●——●

Master planning was a key part of my job. We continually projected out five and ten years, looking for opportunities to upgrade our facilities. One big project we took on was renovating the Twin Wells Golf Course. We planned and budgeted $5 million for a major overhaul of the course and its facilities. To accomplish this, we had to close down the golf course, tell the community and the public about it, and then supervise the work. It was a big project.

While all this was going on, my nephew played well enough at Coppell High School that he landed a full scholarship at the University of Texas as left tackle. I bought season tickets and attended every game in Austin. It was super exciting watching my sister's son compete at a high level.

Then, as if my life could get any better, we watched the NFL draft and saw Connor Williams's name called out in the second round. Yet another miracle occurred when I saw the team making the announcement was our very own Dallas Cowboys. I bought season tickets and watched every game of his rookie season. It's been a wonderful surprise in a life full of them.

●————●

Another key part of being director of parks and recreation was making city council presentations. The meetings were held every two weeks on Thursdays. Everything had to be ready by Monday so the items could be placed on the council's agenda seventy-two hours in advance. If you didn't make the deadline, it didn't get on the agenda. That added time pressure to an already pressurized situation.

At the council meetings, I displayed my requests in PowerPoint slides. I had handled over 400 of these during my career. But I had a great staff behind me putting them all together. This included all the managers for recreation, aquatics, special events, parks, business administration, athletics, and golf.

To get up to speed, I held staff meetings on Tuesdays to see what had been put on the agenda. If I didn't like it or wanted a delay, I simply removed it. During these staff meetings, the managers briefed me on possible questions from the council members. This allowed me to be fully prepared.

To help build up the people coming behind me, occasionally I allowed a manager to give the presentation to the council. This provided them both exposure and experience. Eventually, they gained confidence. It also gave them some appreciation of the grilling I had to endure to get them the items they wanted.

One of the basic tenets of management is having someone able to take over in your absence. It could be an illness or a vacation. If a manager is gone and the person below can't handle the job, that's a reflection of the manager's skills. He or she has not properly trained their subordinates.

I can't emphasize this enough: You've got to have people ready to take over. If I was playing football, it's next man up. He'd better be ready, because I'm not always going to be there.

I put this principle in place when I retired on July 31, 2018. The city of Irving had been great to me. I couldn't have imagined working anywhere else.

I gave them six months to start preparing for my replacement. They bumped up Joe Moses to acting director and conducted a nationwide search. After the dust settled, they selected Joe. It was the right decision.

The folks at Irving decided to have a retirement ceremony for me. Maria Baily, Ramiro Lopez, Joe Moses, and Teresa Kerss helped coordinate and set it up. I invited everyone I could think of. My childhood friend Kyle Jeffery and his wife, Donna, were there. So were Mom, Ninfa, David, Debbie, and Jimmy. Some relatives from South Texas made it: my cousins Sara Vela and Beto Vela and Beto's wife, Mandi, and Beto's daughter Dehra. There were speeches from employees and coworkers. Then I made a speech to thank everyone who had given me a break along with those who had promoted me.

My dad wasn't there because he had died a few years earlier. He had suffered tremendously—my accident, Chonny dying, and divorcing Mom. He retired from the post office and moved to East Texas, where he met a woman. They lived in a trailer together until she was killed in an auto accident. Lung cancer took him shortly after that. It was a tough way to go in a life full of tragedy.

One person I forgot to thank in my retirement speech was Mrs. Dickson. She was my English teacher in eighth grade, writing little notes to me and leaving them on my desk. One day, we were studying

The Diary of Anne Frank. She asked if someone could stand up and read a section to the class. Every student stared down at their desks as the room fell silent. I happened to look up and caught her eye by accident. Of course, she pointed a finger at me. "Come up to the front, Mr. Cerda. I need you to read the first couple of pages out loud to the class because nobody has volunteered."

I didn't have time to say no because I had so much respect for the lady. As I slowly stood up and glanced at my classmates, every face looked scared and in disbelief. They wondered if they were next.

As soon as I started reading, I began expressing the words with my face, like in a play. I didn't have time to be nervous. Even though it was my first time speaking publicly, the words came out smoothly.

I felt like I was up there for maybe thirty seconds, but I was actually reading for five minutes. During the last passage, the bell rang for the next class. Everyone was ready to get out of class and go to the next one. But Mrs. Dickson told everybody to sit down. "Let Mr. Cerda finish."

I hurriedly finished, after which she told me to stick around. When the other students were gone, she said, "Thanks for showing leadership. Always remember that sometimes, you have to show leadership by example."

That was a very powerful concept for an eighth grader to hear. To this day, I've always tried to be a good leader by leading others, even when no one wants to be led.

Later in life, I always made it a point to go by Mrs. Dickson's English class and visit with her. I once told her she'd given me poise and confidence in myself when she made me read that passage. I will never forget Mrs. Dickson and her eighth grade English class. She taught me and my classmates so much.

Sadly, she passed away before seeing the end of my career, what she helped produce. I still have all the notes she gave me. Before she passed, she said she always thought about me. That's heartwarming too.

Here's one of my favorite Mrs. Dickson notes:

"Your days are just beginning. With your spirit, your guts, the doors are just opening for you. Bless you for what you are and the magnificence you will become."

—Mrs. Dickson

Well, Mrs. Dickson, I got the life I didn't expect and the grace from God I didn't deserve. I count myself as one blessed man.

I hope you'd approve.

Thank you!

Cerda's Lessons Learned

I've learned a lot of lessons, some of which might benefit you. Here they are:

1. Your life can change in a heartbeat.
2. Your parents usually do know what's best for you. Listen to them and obey. They should be the most influential people in your life.
3. You are not invincible, no matter how popular, good-looking, athletic, or connected you are.
4. Don't let peer pressure make your decisions for you. Don't be easily influenced. Make sure *you* make your own decisions.
5. When disaster strikes, weather the storm. Get through it. Survive. Then start picking yourself up off the ground.
6. Your faith in God, strong family support, and friends who care about you will help you recover when disaster strikes.
7. Take any opportunity that comes your way, though you will likely have to make your own opportunities.
8. What you know is very important. But who you know will often get you farther. Always stay connected.
9. Give it everything you have to accomplish your goals.
10. You must trust in others.
11. If you bring a problem to me, you'd better have a solution with you because you may not like my solution.
12. Patience is a true virtue.
13. Cherish the good times and enjoy the ride, because it goes too quickly.

The Life I Didn't Expect

a visual look

Ray as an Irving
High School
quarterback.

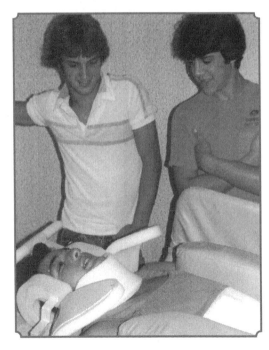

Scott Baxter (*left*)
and Kyle Jeffery
(*right*) try to cheer
up Ray in the
infamous RotaRest
bed.

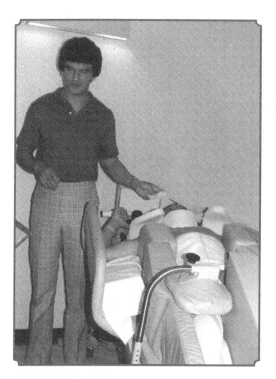

Joel Vela visiting
Ray in the hospital.

A respiratory therapist watches as Ray works on his lung capacity.

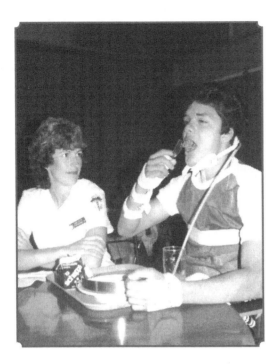

Occupational therapist, Sheri Jones, teaches Ray how to eat.

Ray in physical therapy.

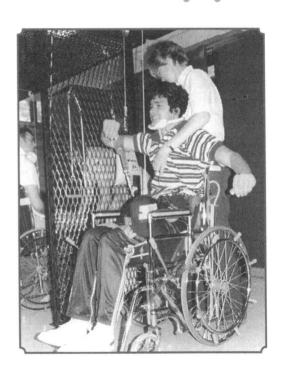

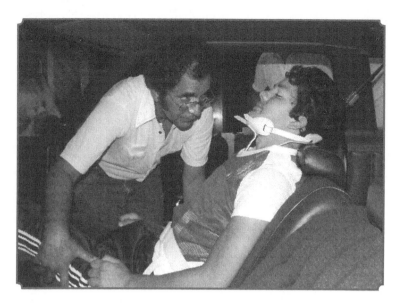

Ray, Sr. in training to transfer his son in and out of a car.

Ray on the sideline watching the Irving High School football game (*Joyce Read Collection*).

Sister Debbie, Mom, and Dad. (*Joyce Read Collection*).

Joyce Read, Ray, and his new van. (*Joyce Read Collection*).

(*Standing left to right*) Brothers David and Chonny, and brother-in-law Jimmy Williams with Ray.

Ninfa with Ray's niece, Nikki.

Epilogue

A formal dedication is located at the front of this book, but I realize some readers might miss it. That's why I've decided to provide more thanks here, where hopefully it's seen and read. Besides, you can never thank people enough. And I'm so grateful for the good-hearted people who have helped me, I just have to say thanks again.

First, I'd like to thank my Lord and Savior. None of this could have been possible without You. Thank You for giving me the power, strength, and courage to complete this book.

When everything else you cling to fails, God is there, waiting for you to have a relationship with Him. Don't exclude Him from your life. My faith in God is what got me through this ordeal.

Just when you think you have it bad, there's always someone else who has it worse than you do. Think about being nailed to a cross. Jesus died for our sins so we could have eternal life in heaven. We simply have to accept God's free grace. Turn to God. He'll never let you down.

To my mom and dad: Thank you for giving your all to me. I know the sacrifices you made. I will forever be in your debt.

To my three siblings, Chonny, Debbie, and David: Thanks for being there for me in one of the most devastating times of my life. I will forever be thankful. I love you.

As kids growing up, my siblings and I woke up to Ninfa tending to our needs. She has been there fifty-two years, raising us kids. She is an angel sent down from heaven. I thank God for her every day.

To Debbie and Jimmy Williams, and Jordyn and Dalton Williams, Morgan and Connor Williams, Lynne and David Cerda, Michael

Ray Cerda, Jr.

Cerda, Elizabeth Minotti, and Nikki and Thomas Daly: I appreciate your support and encouragement through all these years.

●——●

Until much later in life, I never really realized how much I grew up while spending those months in a rehabilitation center. There were many times that I thought to myself, *Will I ever get through this tough time?* It definitely made me a better person. It taught me how to face adversity and overcome many challenges in life.

I learned so much during my stay from the men and women who were injured. I wish I could have kept in touch with them.

I managed to stay positive and concentrate on the things I could accomplish. I knew that if I could deal with this traumatic injury, everything else in life would be easy to conquer. To move forward, I had to have a positive attitude and accept the things I could no longer do. Once I crossed over that mental hurdle, I could focus on succeeding in life. It worked.

Yet, after all the dust settles, I'm still held accountable for my actions. I chose to ride in that vehicle and attend that celebration. I'm responsible for my actions. Me.

The hardworking folks at the rehabilitation center made me realize all this. That's why I'd like to thank the doctors, nurses, occupational, respiratory, and physical therapists, and all those who cared for me during that traumatic time in my life. They taught me to be patient. The tasks I'd previously accomplished in seconds now took minutes or longer. I learned how to adapt and change my life from these people. For that, I'm grateful.

Thank you.

●——●

I have even more people to thank.

To the Irving High School Class of 1982: Thank you for making my life a little easier after my accident.

To my high school football teammates: Thank you for helping me overcome the struggles of facing adversity as a teenager and conquering my mountains. Thank you for your support and encouragement.

To Jan Dickson, Becky Connatser, Steve Hamberger, and Charles Stalcup: Thanks for your guidance.

To Chris Michalski, Tom Henry, Doug Kratz, Nancy Brown, Ron Neely, Dwight Pinnix, Tommy Gonzalez, Ramiro Lopez, Chris Hooper, Victor Conley, and Joe Moses: Thank you for assisting me in continuing to grow and reach my career goals.

To all the Irving parks, recreation, athletics, aquatics, and administration employees: Thank you for doing a tremendous job. Your day-to-day operations did not go unnoticed. I have always said the parks and recreation department has the best employees in the country. I truly believe we had Irving's finest serving our great city.

To Mary and Joel Vela, Joel Enrique Vela, and Cristina Vela Recio: Thank you for your guidance, love, and encouragement.

To Joyce Read: Thank you for making the impossible possible.

To my great friends and relatives: Donna and Kyle Jeffery, Jeff Gibson, Andre Herron, Randy Perkins, Jesse De La Garza, Jimmy Beynon, Cindy Hooper, Daral McKnight, Darrell Cole, Sandra Ansley, Don Smith, Dave Portillo, Medeanna Wilkison, Sheri Jones, James Smith, Melissa and Eli Gross, Jim Wallgren, Arlin White, Laurie Jeffery Beynon, Caroline Green, Buddy Baker, Juliet and Frank Arras, Sr., Michael Arras, Julie Arras, Olivia Ochoa, Maribel and Arturo Indalecio, Ester Vela, Carlos Rodriguez, Sara Vela, Mandi and Beto Vela, Dehra Vela, Lupe Vela, John Hocking and so many others: I thank you for your deep and sincere friendship.

—•—

My oldest brother, Chonny, was someone we all looked up to. He excelled at every sport. Because he was the first one who went to each school—elementary, junior high, and high school—every teacher seemed to know us. There was a ten- or eleven-year period at Irving High with a Cerda somewhere in class. Because Chonny set a great example, we all strived to live up to him. He was a leader, worthy of being looked up to. He was also a good brother. We dearly love and miss him.

—•—

My dad had a vision to better our lives. He felt that for his family to have a richer life, we needed to move from Mission, Texas, to a place that had more jobs, better jobs, and better opportunities. That place was the Dallas/Fort Worth area. I arrived when I was three years old. We settled in Irving. That's where I grew up.

My parents worked so very hard to provide for us. I'm so grateful I could build a house and have Mom live with me.

I still believe Dad missed his calling. He should've been a high school or college coach. He was an excellent mentor and coach, as well as a great tactician. In Little League football, he drew up plays, teaching us offensive and defensive formations. He would even film our football games with a tiny 8mm camera. David and I would study all the formations and plays. Then we'd watch game film from previous games we'd played in.

Dad never played organized sports because he always worked. His family had eleven siblings, so they'd had to work at an early age.

Dad always felt we could excel in sports. Although he never forced them on us, we played sports because we wanted to play. Dad's love for sports was passed down to us kids, along with his good work ethic. He too is badly missed. I love you, Dad.

———•

A few people close to me wanted to say a few things in their own words. Here's my sister, Debbie:

We were kids visiting my maternal grandmother at her house in Mission, Texas. We knew once we were finished there, we'd pile in the car and head to my paternal grandmother's house five miles away. Ray was in middle school and getting impatient. He wanted to go already, telling Dad just that. Dad was in the car with the windows rolled down, but Mom and Grandmother kept talking. Ray couldn't take it. He said, "I'm just going to start running."

So he jumped from the car and started running.

Eventually, Mom climbed in the car and we took off. Somewhere along the road, we caught up to Ray. He was almost there. It was unbelievable. Running at top speed, he'd almost completed the five miles.

Later, I went to Ray's track meets. His feet moved so fast they were spinning. He looked like that cartoon character Road Runner. He was an excellent track star.

My kids have always been his kids. He's like a surrogate parent. They love Ray and call him "Uncle Ray." My kids would run away from home and we'd call Ray. We'd tell him what had happened. Somehow, he knew exactly what to say to them, and he still does. They look up to Ray. They'd call him when we didn't know what to tell them. He's that great with kids.

Here is my brother David:

Growing up as kids, I remember Ray being competitive in everything he did. Our family was gifted with athleticism, so sports were always a part of Ray. I could tell early on in life that Ray was going to be a leader in whatever he chose to do. He had that charismatic personality that great leaders tend to possess, and people tend to gravitate toward.

I saw the competitive nature in Ray follow him into adulthood. Even after his accident, I saw his competitive, strong-willed nature shine through while he went to rehab. He never wanted an electric wheelchair to move him around. And he never wanted anyone to feel bad for him for what he was going through. I think that, along with his faith, was what kept his drive alive.

He's never been one to take the easy road. Ray believed that by putting in the hard work to get through whatever lay ahead, it would lead him to success. It's no surprise to me that Ray has always been in some type of leadership role throughout his life. Good leaders leave a lasting impression on people they come in contact with.

It's not unusual that I run into someone and tell them my name, and they ask if I'm related to Ray. I say he's my brother. That tells you the impact he's had on them.

Competitive spirit and a leader.

That's my brother.

Here's my brother-in-law, Jimmy:

I met Debbie after Ray's accident. They told me the whole story about what had happened. Everything. But you don't realize the impact of all that when you're in your early twenties.

I hung out with Ray a lot. He was never a victim, so he handled it real well. When you're not a victim, it helps other people not feel sorry for you. I know it bothered him from time to time, but he dealt with it. I think it took three or four years, maybe even five, for him to come to grips with it. Then he took off.

Ninfa's an angel. She was there when I moved in. I remember them trying to fix her up and introduce her to guys, but Ninfa didn't want any of that. She told me many years ago that she thinks she was put here because Ray was going to have his accident.

Ninfa's a very interesting person. She doesn't sleep very much. She probably gets about four or five hours a night. You can go over there at three in the morning and she'll be up watching TV or something. I don't know how much of that is Ninfa and how much of that is just the lifestyle that's developed from Ray being in a chair.

When you hear the family saying, "Ninfa's an angel," they mean she's an angel. She never sits down. She never relaxes. She never wants to do anything for herself. I've got friends that told me, "If I could steal Ninfa, I would."

Ray is great with our kids. I'm a big proponent of it takes a village to raise a kid. I think kids should have their own relationships. I think for the most part, your family is probably the safest people for your kids talk to. You don't need to be filtering the relationships your kids have with uncles and aunts and people like that.

If I had a problem with my kids—like when they were nine or ten years old and they quit listening to me, or we were getting on each other's nerves or fighting—I told them, "Go visit Ray. Go over there and see Grandma and Ninfa." That wasn't hard to do, because they loved Ninfa as much as everybody else did, so they'd go over there.

My kids are huge in Ray's life right now. After all, my son Connor was named after Ray—Connor Ray Williams.

Ray keeps up with them. He's loves following Connor's football, and Dalton's coaching, and Morgan's career. That gives him a lot of meaning in his life right now.

My kids are as close to his own kids as he's probably ever going to get. It's a very relaxed relationship. Ray loves my kids. They hug him every time they see him.

It's hard to separate Ray from the chair. One thing I can tell you about Ray that I really like is Ray is very objective because of his view from the chair. In some ways, it's kind of isolated him from the world. He doesn't carry the baggage that Debbie and I do.

I always go talk to Ray when I want an unbiased opinion about something, because he doesn't have anything to skew his view of the world. Ray provides solid advice. He's been sitting in that chair his whole life, just looking at the world around him, studying it.

Ray gives you his unvarnished, unbiased opinion. Some people don't like it because he's so direct and doesn't sugarcoat. I love it.

He's lived the last thirty-eight years in a chair, since he was sixteen years old. He doesn't want to hear about your troubles. If he can overcome what he overcame and do with his life what he did, then you don't have an excuse for not doing it too.

His accident affected me. It makes me realize how fragile life is, that I've got to be careful. When I raised my kids, I used Ray as an example. More than anything, there's no whining. I don't like whining anyway. I don't like victims and, boy, Ray has really strengthened that in me. I probably would've felt like that anyway, but he's given me even more resolve in that area.

Christmas is big for Ray. He also likes our Thanksgivings. We always do the circle at Thanksgiving. He insists on it as most of us do. Some don't like it, but he's the one who says, "Let's do it."

The circle at Thanksgiving is where we get in a big circle, everybody holds hands, and one by one, everybody says what they're thankful for. He's usually the only one who doesn't cry. Everybody else is crying.

He's sincere about what he's thankful for, but he holds his emotions in very well. In fact, I don't think I've ever seen Ray cry. He's a strong individual. After what he's been through, you aren't going to break him. If he was going to be broken, he was going to be broken a long time ago. He keeps a lot of things inside.

Ray doesn't like flowers. We always plant flowers at our house. I offered to Ray, "Let me plant you some flowers." He doesn't like them because they die. He hates seeing the cycle of life do its thing. It's one reason I don't plant flowers for him.

The flowers are beautiful, but eventually they die.

Here's Kyle Jeffery:

Ray's situation has bonded me and my wife. We're so thankful to be together, to have one another. We occasionally go to dinner with Ray, and it's really sad when we drive home. I give him a hug and a kiss, tell him I love him. He drives away alone. It's hard. I get emotional every time he drives away. My wife does too. She gets emotional just because I do.

He's a star. He's someone that everybody should have in their lives.

I've got six kids, so I'm kid-rich. I have the best litter of kids around. I had to make up for Ray's.

My kids look up to Ray. They love him, and they all know him very well. When we go to dinner, the kids come with us. They're like, "Is Ray coming?"

I'll say, "Yeah, Ray is coming with us," and they get excited. They're inspired by him.

After the accident, it was hard for me. It still is. It's made me be more grateful for what I have. It's made me proud of him. He has been through so much adversity yet he keeps his head up, inspiring so many people. He's all about giving. But thank God that it happened to him instead of someone who couldn't handle it.

•———•

I wrote this book to help others who are in my situation. I hope to motivate and tell them that they can overcome everything. It's not the end of the world. The sun will come out tomorrow. You can still be a productive citizen and have fulfillment in life. I'm living proof!

I'm currently retired after working at my thirty-year municipality career. I'm consulting in the parks and recreation field. I also speak to groups about these topics:

a. My life experiences as a handicapped person;
b. Motivational topics;
c. How my spiritual beliefs got me through; and
d. This book, *The Life I Didn't Expect*.

Should you be interested in having me speak to your group, please contact me at RayCerdaBook@Gmail.com.

I can't wait to hear from you!

Author Bio

In 1982, Ray Cerda, Jr. convinced a man to let him coach track athletes—from a wheelchair! He had no idea this summer job would lead to a career that reached the highest levels of a large city in Texas.

Eventually, he managed hundreds of employees and millions of dollars in parks and recreation—all from a wheelchair.

Ray retired in 2018 with over 30 years in city government and now consults in the parks and recreation field. He is also available for public speaking events—both life story and motivational subjects.

His wheelchair prevents him from doing nothing. This is his first book. Contact Ray at RayCerdaBook@Gmail.com.